TOGETHER
WE WERE
ELEVEN FOOT NINE

TOGETHER
WE WERE
ELEVEN FOOT NINE

The Twenty-Year Friendship
of Hall of Fame Pitcher Jim Palmer
and Orioles Manager Earl Weaver

by

JIM PALMER
and Jim Dale

Andrews and McMeel

A Universal Press Syndicate Company
Kansas City

Designed by Barrie Maguire

Library of Congress Cataloging-in-Publication Data

Palmer, Jim, 1945–
    Together we were eleven foot nine : the twenty-year friend-
ship of Hall of Fame pitcher Jim Palmer and Orioles manager
Earl Weaver / by Jim Palmer and Jim Dale.
        p. cm.
    ISBN 0-8362-0781-5 (hardcover)
    1. Palmer, Jim, 1945– . 2. Baseball players—United
States—Biography. 3. Weaver, Earl, 1930– . 4. Baseball
managers—United States—Biography. 5. Baltimore Orioles
(Baseball team)—History. I. Dale, Jim, 1948– . II. Title.
GV865.P3A3 1996
796.352'092—dc20
    [B]   95–42235
                                                            CIP

Every effort has been made to give appropriate credit to photographers whose photos have been used in this book. If a photograph lacks proper credit, please inform the publisher for correction in future editions.

Attention: Schools and Businesses

Andrews and McMeel books are available at quantity discounts with bulk purchase for educational, business, or sales promotional use. For information, please write to: Special Sales Department, Andrews and McMeel, 4900 Main Street, Kansas City, Missouri 64112.

Contents

Acknowledgments

Under the heading of I Couldn't Have Done It without You, Earl Weaver tops the list. Thanks for enough memories to fill a book.

Thanks to the Orioles, Cal Sr., Jim Russo, Bamby, Rabbit, Crazy Horse, the Robinsons, the Macs, Flanny, Turkey, Robin, and all the talented and classy players, coaches, and front-office personnel that made up baseball's winningest organization from 1965 to 1984. Many thanks to Charles Steinberg and the Orioles public-relations office for their invaluable information and assistance.

Max, thanks for choosing to be my dad. To my daughters, Jamie and Kelly, and to my stepson, P.J., who became my son, I appreciate all your love and overwhelming support. All of my gratitude to my wife, Joni, for her inspiration and undying patience in hearing me repeat my favorite stories so often that we finally convinced ourselves, coauthor Jim Dale, a literary agent, and a publisher that we had the makings of a book.

—Jim Palmer

Without Jim Palmer, his remarkable career, his equally remarkable memory, and our mutual weakness for Italian food, there'd be no book. So, thanks for telling me the first of many 'Jim and Earl' stories, in flawless detail, over a plate of pasta one night. And thanks for giving me the chance to be "the short, curly haired guy sitting next to Jim Palmer."

Thanks to Mel Berger, our agent, to Stuart Friedel, full-time Oriole fan and occasional attorney, to Donna Martin, our editor, to Joni, to Kristin, and to Barbara. And thanks to my son, Andy, who let me use all of his baseball reference books and who explained baseball "stuff" to his father very patiently.

—Jim Dale

Preface

Jim Palmer was an impressive rookie in 1965 with the Baltimore Orioles. In 1966, he won fifteen games and shutout the Dodgers 6–0 in the World Series.

Then, in '67, he hurt his arm and was sent to Rochester in Triple A, not so much to see if he could work out the injury as to see if he could ever be a major league pitcher again.

Earl Weaver had knocked around the minor leagues as a coach and manager for years. He won games and he found talent, but he couldn't seem to make it to the big leagues. In 1967 he was managing the Rochester Red Wings in Triple A when a kid with a sore arm came down. Weaver wasn't optimistic about the pitcher's future.

Needless to say, the kid's sore arm healed, and the manager made it to the majors.

From 1969 to 1982, Jim Palmer and Earl Weaver were Baltimore Orioles together. They were as different as they come. Tall and short, cerebral and visceral, handsome and, well, not so handsome. They rarely agreed on anything and almost never on baseball. They fought, moaned, bitched, contradicted, joked, jibed, jabbed, teased, taunted, and second-guessed each other publicly and privately. On the mound and on the golf course. In the locker room and in the press.

All the two of them could seem to do in harmony was win baseball games.

Palmer won three Cy Young Awards, four Gold Gloves, had eight seasons with twenty or more wins, appeared in five All-Star games, and was elected to the Hall of Fame the first year he was eligible. Weaver won 1,480 games, finishing first or second in twelve of sixteen seasons. His Orioles won their division six times, went to the World Series four times, and won it in 1970.

Palmer and Weaver. Together. Was it coincidence or providence? Maybe they'd have been just as good if they'd never met. Never hollered, never thrown shoes or banged lockers, never threatened to quit or get traded, never shouted, never pouted, never broke down crying or laughing, never cared that much about winning or agonized that much over losing, never understood each other so well. Maybe they'd have been as good or maybe not. We won't ever know.

What we do know is, together they were phenomenal. Flint against stone, the sparks it takes to make fire. Season after season, it was a love-hate-win relationship.

—Jim Dale

Introduction: Me and Earl

We're pretty different, me and Earl. And then again, we aren't.

A pitcher and a manager.

A kid who was raised on Park Avenue and a guy who was brought up in St. Louis on the bad side of a street where even the good side isn't too good.

An analyzer and a shouter.

One guy who housecleans for relaxation and another who's been called "walking dirt."

A tall jock who modeled underwear and a sawed-off fireplug who wasn't a pretty sight even with all his clothes on.

Palmer and Weaver.

I was eighteen and I knew that I knew pretty much everything there was to know. He was thirty-two and he knew he sure as hell couldn't learn anything from an eighteen-year-old know-it-all.

I had a photographic memory or close to it. Earl scribbled stats, piles and piles of figures and percentages on everybody and everything. All those sheets with all those numbers made him a better manager. Although he could have just asked me.

They say I had injuries to muscles other pitchers didn't know they had. I asked Earl to take me out of ballgames even though we were winning and I was still throwing the ball over the plate. Because some muscle somewhere hurt.

Earl would've never taken himself out of a ballgame. He'd play hurt. Then again, since he was a lousy player, it wouldn't have made a difference.

I moved the players around the field when I was pitching, and it didn't exactly build a close bond between us. I'd just figure the batter was going to hit to the right so they ought to move right. It made sense. And I was right enough times to make it worth it.

Earl said, "If I was his teammate, I'd hit him in the face."

(Warm guy.) But when I shifted the outfield, Earl didn't shift it back.

Winning. That's what we shared. It was blood to both of us. Sure, you figure everybody who plays pro sports wants to win. And they do. But they aren't all prisoners of winning. They aren't ruled and wrenched by it. They don't stare at ceilings all night imagining batting orders. Or wind directions. They don't close their eyes and see replays of errors. Or pitches that missed the corner.

A few do. Losing is pain. Winning is medicine. It's the only thing that makes losing go away.

Some of us go at it with method and analysis and obsession. That's me. I can think my way into and out of anything and everything. Maybe to a fault.

Some go at with bared teeth and flailing arms and obsession. That's Earl. He tears a game apart like it's raw flesh. His mind is spinning through statistics while his body is whirling and charging and heaving. He'll do anything to win.

I thought I could outthink him any day. But he could out–*wanna win* anybody, everyday.

Did we ever become friends? Yeah. Finally. Not like somebody you share things with. Not like someone who you turn to for advice. The day Earl puts his arm around you, it's because he thinks you've got a piece of steak caught in your throat and he's going to do the Heimlich maneuver . . . but only if you're in the lineup that day.

We're friends. We understand each other. We respect each other. He knew when I said I was hurt, I was hurt. I knew he knew how to manage. I knew he'd spit in an umpire's face just to get us charged up. (I knew I never wanted to be an umpire.)

He's stubborn. So am I. We disagreed on everything. So, with everything out of the way, now we don't disagree anymore.

We understand each other. I know just what's wrong with him and he knows what's wrong with me. Except he's wrong about me.

This is about us.

TOGETHER
WE WERE
ELEVEN FOOT NINE

1965 to '67
The Pre-Earl Years

**Life was peaceful. Life was good.
I didn't even know anybody named
Earl Weaver existed.
It's like Joni Mitchell sang,
"You don't know what you've got
till it's gone."**

Jim Palmer was born in New York City on October 15, 1945. He never knew his real parents and was adopted as an infant by Polly and Moe Wiesen. Jim and his sister lived on Park Avenue in Manhattan. He first learned to throw a baseball in Central Park, with the butler.

When Jim was nine, Moe died. Polly moved the family to Southern California. There she met and married Max Palmer, a character actor and shoe salesman. Jim played Little League baseball for the Beverly Hills Yankees. He pitched, played the outfield, and hit home runs.

A few years later, the Palmers moved to Scottsdale, Arizona. Jim graduated from high school in 1964 with All-State honors in football, basketball, and baseball and a 3.4 grade point average. He had full scholarship offers from USC, UCLA, and Arizona State University, as well as a partial scholarship offer from Stanford. He would have played basketball at UCLA with a guy then named Lew Alcindor, now known as Kareem Abdul-Jabbar.

Jim was pursued by major league baseball teams as a slugging outfielder and as a pitcher. In the summer of 1963, he pitched minor league ball in Winner, South Dakota. At the end of the summer, he signed with the Baltimore Orioles.

What I Wanted to Be
When (and If) I Grew Up

Jim-Palmer-the-Pitcher. It's like one long word to a lot of baseball fans. *Jim-Palmer-the-Pitcher.* Like that's what I was meant to be. Like it was fated. God said, "Okay, I think I'll make that guy a pitcher." What else could *Jim-Palmer-the-Pitcher* be? Well, lots of things, maybe.

When I got out of high school, I wasn't even sure I wanted to play baseball. And I sure wasn't sure I wanted to be a pitcher. I just loved to play. Anything. (I still do.) I loved to field and I loved to hit. I hit pretty well, too. Part of it, I guess, was knowing about pitching. I kind of knew what was coming at me and when to swing and where and when not to.

And then there was football and basketball. I loved them, too. I was All-State in football and led the state in scoring in basketball. And I had never had to make a choice. To play one position and not another or one sport and give up the others. I just played everything I could.

Of course, I did see these guys getting really big bonuses to play baseball right from school. Like Bob Bailey in 1964. He got $225,000 from Pittsburgh. And Bob Garabaldi who got $175,000 coming out of college. That part made baseball pretty attractive. But by the time I graduated from high school, major league teams had shut down the big bonuses, at least for a while. (I'm sure they weren't colluding. It must have been a coincidence that they all stopped paying big bonuses on the very same day.) They still recruited. They just did it with skinnier, cheaper, crummier wallets.

I got scouted starting when I was fourteen or fifteen years old. By the time I was seventeen, they were saying, "Mrs. Palmer, your boy throws the ball ninety-seven miles an hour." And Mrs. Palmer would smile.

I was 10–0. I was having games where I'd face twenty-one

guys and eighteen would go down on strikes. I got scholarship offers from Southern Cal and some others. I had good grades so I got into Stanford with a partial scholarship because they don't give full rides. And I was offered $15,000 or $20,000 to go straight into baseball. The skinny-wallet bonus.

I figured, okay, I'll either go to USC or UCLA and play basketball *and* baseball or go to Stanford, except I didn't want my parents to have to pay if I could go for nothing. Or maybe I'd go to Arizona State, fifteen miles away in Tempe.

Arizona State had a great baseball team and a great coach, Bobby Winkles, and they had won the NCAA championship the year before. He came to see me and said, "You're too good for the American Legion teams around here. You won't get any better playing with them. I've got five guys who go to ASU going up to the college league in South Dakota. I want you to go up there."

So, I go. Remember, I'm seventeen, and at seventeen you don't think you're being faced with making a rational career decision. You think, you're just playing another sport in another season and, hey, you'll see what happens. (Which, it turns out, is not a bad way to go through life, since rational career decisions rarely get decided rationally anyway, but that'll become pretty clear as my not-so-rational career goes on.) So, I drive my little red Corvair up to Winner, South Dakota.

Everybody else up there is older than I am, nineteen or twenty. Very mature. There are 2,500 people in Winner (which leads everybody who's ever been there and escaped to the obvious jokes about how many losers are in Winner). Now to satisfy the NCAA inspectors, we're supposed to work during the day and play ball at night. And we get $300 a month. But nobody really had a job. Five of us lived in this basement apartment with a game warden living above us. There are four girls in town, two restaurants, one movie, no TV, no air-conditioning, and the temperature is always about a hundred.

We'd go to sleep at four A.M. and get up at noon and the game warden would take us out to shoot prairie dogs for sport. The prairie dogs always lost.

One day the assistant manager of the team comes to our door sometime before noon and says, "The NCAA inspector's coming so you guys have to go to your jobs."

In unison, me and my four more mature, experienced roommates say, "What jobs?"

He says, "Palmer, you're on the grounds crew. Tony Alessi, you work for the park. Tom Hamm, you're the lifeguard at the pool. . . ."

So we go to our "jobs," which we're not particularly good at since we've never done them before. And the inspector comes around. He's sitting in his car up on top of this bowl that rings the field below, just like the cars sit up there every night to watch games and flash their lights and honk their horns. (This is a little town that lives for baseball.) And he's watching us trip over the rakes and pretend to study the rocks in the outfield and taste the lime to make sure it's not "lemon."

Then he goes to the pool and asks if Tom Hamm is the lifeguard. The woman who runs it says, "No, but he's a darn fine swimmer and a nice boy. I'm sure if someone was drowning, he'd help them."

So now the inspector goes to the little restaurant in town which the part-owner of the team also part-owns, and he sees about half the team in there having lunch, which on our schedule was breakfast. He gets the whole picture and the NCAA cracked down after that. We really had to do our jobs. Kind of.

But the team is good. This is real baseball. Bobby Floyd, our shortstop, ended up playing for the Orioles. Merv Rettenmund, who is now a hitting instructor with San Diego, hit over .300 with the Orioles in '70 and '71, and he was my catcher and also played in the outfield. Carl Morton went to the big leagues. Jim Lonborg, from Stanford, won the Cy Young Award in 1967. We had five or six guys go on to major league careers.

But, at the moment, we're in a best-of-three playoff. I'm supposed to pitch the third game, if there is one. We lose the first game, 1–0. Okay, what's the incentive to win the championship? Even at the lowest level, you've got to have a carrot. A ring. A bonus. A trophy. An award. A ceremony. Or, in this case . . . mileage. Yes, mileage. A gas allowance. If we lose, we get nine cents a mile for the drive home. If we win, we get thirteen cents a mile. So, to get four cents a mile, we have to stay in four-girl, two-restaurant, no–air-conditioning, no TV, hundred-degree, dead–prairie dog, Winner, South Dakota, for an extra week. Some incentives don't work as well as others.

It's Game 2 in Sturgis, South Dakota (which may be Winner's illegitimate sister city). And, if we're lucky enough to win the second game, we get to stay and play the third one right there in lovely Sturgis (where we can meet *their* four girls).

Harry Dalton, who's a farm director for the Orioles, has driven all the way there (I wonder how much *he* got per mile) to see me pitch that third game. But it doesn't look like there's going to be a third game because in the second game (1) we're already behind, (2) the bases are loaded, and (3) the three best hitters in the league are coming up. We're facing the harsh reality of losing, of only getting nine cents a mile, and of being forced to leave lovely Sturgis and Winner and anyplace else that ends in "Dakota." We're distraught. Okay, maybe we're ecstatic.

I pitch one inning of the game and strike out the first two batters. The third one grounds out to the shortstop, and Harry Dalton decides I'm one of the guys the Orioles want to sign. We lose and I win.

Now we drive back from Sturgis to Winner in the three team station wagons and get there at about 5:30 in the morning. We go to the team owner's restaurant for breakfast, get our $300 for our "jobs" plus our nine cents a mile, and the five guys from Arizona State head out for the 1,300-mile drive to Scottsdale. Skip Hancock, who later got an $80,000 bonus from the Dodgers, has two other guys in his Ford Falcon, and I've got me and Louie Lagunis, an All-American second baseman, in my red Corvair.

We drive and drive and drive some more. Sixteen, seventeen hours. Mostly Louie is sleeping and I'm driving. Finally, about three hundred miles from Phoenix, around the Four Corners, Louie says, "You sleep, I'll drive." It must be about 7:30 in the morning, so we'd been up for almost two days counting our escape from Sturgis. But we're young and we can do anything. Plus we don't waste a lot of time on stuff like thinking.

Louie is driving . . . and I'm half-awake . . . and it's open range . . . and we're on an elevated highway with no fences and cattle crossings . . . and I'm half-asleep . . . and Bobby Vinton is singing "Blue Velvet" on the radio. . . .

And my eyes click open. We're going sideways at sixty miles an hour across the left lane, headed right over the side of the highway into I-don't-know-where. Louie is asleep. I grab the wheel to jerk it back. Louie wakes up and grabs it. Too late. The car careens off the road, rolls and bounces and flips down into this gully. There are no seat belts, so my head hits the ceiling and we roll over three times and now we're upside down, in the backseat of the red Corvair along with our golf clubs and suitcases.

I say, "Louie, are you all right?"

And he says, sort of groggy, "Yeah. You?"

I say, "I'm fine," but I don't really know since I hit my head three times. There's this little twelve-inch window in the back, and I try to crawl out.

In the meantime, Skip and his guys have pulled up and jumped out to get us. I cut my knee and Louie cut his arm.

And this Indian on a horse rides by and Skip asks him if he'll trade a demolished car with crushed doors, no windshield, and bent wheels for his horse. No deal.

Finally, this other guy rides up and gets the car, or whatever Ralph Nader would call it at that point, towed to some burial ground, and we hop in Skip's car and drive to Phoenix. I call my mother, get stitched up, and finally go home.

I'm soaking in the bathtub with this massive headache and massive knee ache and in come these guys from the Astros. Right into the bathroom. Paul Richards, who ran the Houston ball club (and was once the GM of the Orioles) had a guy who was like a spy and knew everything, including the fact that we were home early and I'm soaking in the tub and probably what color our bathroom tiles were. Richards walks right into the bathroom and says, "I got two contracts for you. One is for $50,000 and one is for $45,000 with a college scholarship. Both have progressive bonuses."

I say, "Can you hand me that towel?" and sort of limp out of the tub.

He says, "What happened?"

My mom says, very motherly and nonthreatening, "Oh, the boys had a little car accident, but they're fine."

He shrugs it off and goes right into the living room and takes my mom's putter and practices on the carpet, making himself comfortable. He was like that. He just did things his way. (Like that past summer when he wanted to see me play a game but had to leave town by a certain time, so he convinced the league to actually move a night game up to day game just to meet his schedule. As it turned out I pitched a 5–2 win and hit a home run.)

So there he is, putting, and he says, "Which contract do you want?" Like I'm going to sign with him while I'm soaking wet with a towel around me and not talk to anybody else. I almost did.

But I had twelve other teams call on me. One was the Orioles. Jim Russo (who signed Boog Powell and Dave McNally) and Jim Wilson come over and they're the opposite of Paul Richards. Very polite and very "So nice to see you, Mr. and Mrs. Palmer."

They leave and my mother says, "Jimmy, you should sign with the Orioles."

That's how it is when you're seventeen. You're a kid who just likes to throw and hit a baseball and thinks it's fun to run with a football and shoot jumpshots on a basketball court, and three months later you play ball with guys who are older and better and you have a car accident that nearly kills you and then a dozen guys from the pros show up on your doorstep offering you something called a "contract" and the chance to play major league baseball. One of the guys your mom says is really nice. And he thinks you should pitch. That's how you make rational career decisions. That's how you become *Jim-Palmer-the-Pitcher.*

Here's the PS. I go to ASU and sign up for ROTC. I bend down to shine my shoes, bump my knee, and it swells up like a cantaloupe. I tell Jim Russo, who says to have it operated on by the best orthopedic guy in the state and then don't tell him any more about it.

And I still see Louie Lagunis every so often. He told his kids he knew me and they didn't believe him. He says, "Honest kids, I almost killed Jim Palmer in a car accident."

When I see him, I don't think, That's the guy I almost died with. I think, that's Louie Lagunis, who could really hit a low fastball.

That's how baseball is. And baseball is what I picked. Or it picked me.

The Toughest Guy I Ever Pitched against Was Sherwin Williams

In 1965, I came in to relieve Dave McNally against the Yankees, hit a two-run home run off Jim Bouton, and won my first major league game, 7–5.

In 1966, I was twenty, playing for the Orioles, and I pitched a 6–0 shutout in the World Series. It was against a legend named Sandy Koufax. I was the youngest pitcher to pitch a shutout in a World Series game.

We won the championship. I'd never even met anyone named Earl Weaver. I was on my way. It was sweet. And it was short-lived.

The next spring I couldn't throw a baseball. I don't mean I couldn't throw the ball fast. Or I couldn't throw the ball accurately. Not ninety-five miles an hour, or eighty-five, or five. Not high and outside or low and inside or anywhere on any side. Not a gently breaking ball or a totally broken ball. Nothing. And everything hurt.

Why, I don't know. But I spent roughly the next twenty years, along with every M.D. from orthopedists to neurologists to veterinarians, trying to find out. The closest I can figure was that it was the northeast wall of the second bedroom of a ranch house in Baltimore County. We should've left it "eggshell white."

My then-wife, Susie, and I bought a house in '66 in Baltimore. We were going to have a family and settle down. Jamie, our first daughter, was going to be born in November, so we were getting the house ready. I'm making $7,500, which meant we could barely afford the down payment, which meant we sure couldn't afford to hire anybody to do anything, which meant that left me to work on the house after games and on off days. In fact, we couldn't afford furniture except a bed and a sofa and a kitchen table.

After a game, I'd work on the lawn (which I still love to do) or do some wiring (which I am now terrified of doing) or paint a wall (which I'm now smart enough not to do). The house was one of those where they sell it to you painted one color everywhere. Naturally, we wanted to make it ours and our colors. I'd come home and get a fresh roller and mix up a gallon of Sherwin Williams "misty aqua" or "sunset amber" or "depressing hailstorm."

I'd look into the paint for a sign it was ready, stretch down into the pan, dip the roller in for the paint, wind up, reach high, thrust that roller out, and rooooll the paint down the wall. Again and again. That roller, heavy with paint, down the wall. Heavier and heavier. Roll after roll. Fast rolls. Down the middle. Nothing wild. Pitch a night, paint a night. Me versus Sherwin Williams. No drips. No errors. Until every bit of that "eggshell white" was . . . shut out.

Pretty soon, the house looked real nice. And I'd have waved my arm at it proudly . . . if I could have lifted my arm.

My arm started to hurt a lot. I got introduced to cortisone injections. They eased the pain temporarily. Just enough to pitch and win some games. And to pitch in the World Series. I got an extra $11,683.04 for the championship. But the house was already painted by then.

By the time spring training came, I was sore all the time. I held out for a bigger contract . . . from $7,500 to their first offer of $13,500 to my wanting $17,000 to settling for $15,000 . . . and using the time to hope and pray my arm would stop hurting. But it didn't.

I couldn't throw a ball. I couldn't raise my arm. I couldn't lower my arm. I couldn't release. Every time I went into my windup, I could feel that roller going up and coming down the wall. Heavier and heavier. That's how my arm felt in 1967. Heavy.

I got off to a so-so start that ended up being the high

point of my year. Finally, I'm pitching in Fenway Park. The first guy up hits the first pitch for a double. The second guy up hits the first pitch for single. The third guy up, Don Demeter, hits the first pitch for a home run.

Hank Bauer comes out to the mound and asks Andy Etchebarren, the catcher, who had one long eyebrow across both eyes, "How's Palmer throwing?"

One Brow says, "How would I know? I haven't caught one yet."

Bauer motioned to the bullpen and the minor leagues all in one gesture.

The next day I'm on my way to Triple A, where I'm going to play for Earl Weaver. The doctors each had a different name for what I had. It later turned out to be something called biceptal tendonitis. They could call it whatever they want. I just knew when it came to guys named Williams, I'd rather face Ted than Sherwin.

1968 and '69
A Preview of Coming Attractions

I met Earl Weaver in Rochester, New York. He seemed pleasant enough. Then we went onto the baseball field.

After finishing 1966 by winning Game 2 of the World Series, Jim Palmer's arm started hurting and didn't stop for the next two years. He started the following season with the Orioles but went into a downward spiral that sent him from one minor league team to another, from Rochester to the Instructional League. It was in Rochester, in 1967, that he had his first, fateful encounter with Earl Weaver. The meeting was prophetic. But it didn't result in a victory or an improvement in Jim's sore arm.

In 1967, things went downhill, and 1968 started out on the same path. The arm pain got worse instead of better. Jim was ready to give up and go back to college. He agreed to go to Puerto Rico for one last try.

It was there that things turned around.

In the meantime, the Orioles had moved Earl Weaver up to the majors and, in mid-'68, up to manager.

Once Upon a Time in Rochester

I met Earl Weaver in 1967. I had been sent down to Rochester in the International League for rehabilitation, and Earl was managing the Red Wings. I'd heard about him. Hell, kids who played catch with ice balls in the Russian tundra had heard of Earl. But I hadn't "experienced" him, and he hadn't experienced me.

Of course, I respected the guy. He was the manager. He won ball games. I was a nobody. And I had been sent down, not up. So, I was in a pretty humble position.

I'd seen those old movies about the talented but raw kid who meets the crusty but wise manager who changes the kid's life. I could be that kid. I knew just how it would go. Earl would watch me and watch me and then, very dramatically, with a sound track full of violins building in the background, he'd saunter over and make the slightest change in my motion or my delivery or maybe he'd say . . . dramatically . . . just the right thing and the music would swell to a crescendo . . . and I'd become the greatest pitcher of all time. I was ready to do my part.

We were ahead 6–0 and my arm was feeling pretty decent. But I'm facing some tough batters. Particularly one named Bench, as in Johnny. I had managed to strike him out the first time. But now I had given up a hit and two walks and Bench is up again. Imagine being twenty-one years old and coming up against a guy like that. I look at him. He looks at me. His look is a lot more intimidating than my look.

And then it happened.

I swear I heard the movie sound track start up. And there, with the sun at his back, like a western hero, out comes a stocky, determined man. Earl and me at the mound. The music gets louder. The crowd gets quieter. Earl looks at me and says, "Throw him a fastball down the middle."

I'm a little surprised since I thought Johnny Bench prayed

every night for fastballs, down the middle. But this is the moment. Earl is the man. I'm the kid.

The music is really loud now. I nod. Earl nods. The whole crowd nods.

I wind up and I throw a fastball, down the middle. It's fast and it's down the middle, the two characteristics required in a fastball down the middle. It's not just fast. It's not just down the middle. It's both. It's just what the crusty but wise manager who would change my life wanted me to throw.

It was also just what Johnny Bench wanted me to throw. He hit it out of the park. Four hundred and fifty feet. A grand slam. His prayers had been answered. God sent me to Johnny Bench.

I learned a lot from Earl Weaver. The first thing I learned was that he didn't know a thing about pitching.

Rats

I thought 1967 was the beginning of the end of one of the shortest promising careers in major league baseball, although not the only one of its kind. Everybody in the game knows some guy who was a phenomenon for a season or who hit every pitch for a month or threw a hundred-mile-an-hour no-hitter one afternoon and then faded away to become an insurance rep in Columbus who is now known as a guy who *almost* made it in the majors. I could see the future, and it didn't include free shirts with my name on the back and unlimited towels.

First I had been sent to Triple A, where I met Earl Weaver and learned how he motivated by the positive-negative approach (Don't fuck up! Stop fucking up! At least, fuck up less!) and found out what he knew about pitching ("throw sliders") and what he didn't know about pitching ("throw Johnny Bench a fastball, down the middle").

Then it was Miami with Cal Ripken Sr., who had been my first manager in Aberdeen, South Dakota. He welcomed me with open arms, which was something I couldn't do with my arms since the right one was killing me.

From there it was back to Rochester for a guy named Billy Demars, who didn't want to rehabilitate players like me; he wanted to win the Triple A title and get the hell out of Rochester.

Then I went to Elmira, New York, with Ripken again, where I threw a pitch, heard a pop, and told Cal it was a part of my body that probably shouldn't make that kind of tire-blowout noise.

Next stop, Clearwater, Florida, in the Instructional League, where just about any team that had the money could pick me up and exactly none of them stepped forward. I leafed through a brochure about a summer course in insurance sales they were offering in Columbus.

But George Bamberger, who was the minor league pitching coach, said the Orioles wanted me to go to Puerto Rico in the Winter League. This seemed like a really bad idea, worse than a high fastball to Johnny Bench. I had moved steadily downward since early '67, and now he wants me to go to Puerto Rico in '68, where they play real baseball, with real players, who are on their way up, not down, and they much prefer winning to having the other team get ten or twelve runs off the starting pitcher in the first three innings (my new specialty).

I go home to think. I go to the hospital, where they tell me the muscle behind my shoulder has healed. Great news! But I've strained a tendon in my right arm. Rotten news.

I go to a Bullets basketball game, sit next to a pharmaceutical rep named Marv Foxxman who tells me about an anti-inflammatory drug called Indocin, and since I'd even tried butazoladine, the drug they give horses, I get some of this stuff from Marv and I try it.

And then, I'm off to Santurce, Puerto Rico.

Bamberger is there when I report and he watches me

throw the ball. The ball is doing an interesting thing. It's leaving my hand, after my arm has flung it forward, at about ninety-five miles an hour, and it is going where it's supposed to go, the inside corner or outside corner or dropping off the table, none of which it has done for a long time. Maybe it's not the ball. Maybe it's me. The guy who was destined for Mutual of Omaha.

Bamberger says, "That's the best I've seen you throw in two years."

And I say, because I just realize it for the first time, "My arm doesn't hurt anymore." And it doesn't. Just like that.

It's December of 1968 and Frank Robinson is managing the team and we have some terrific guys, like I said, guys who like to win. We have Elrod Hendricks catching, who ends up leading the league in home runs along with our Gold Glove first baseman, George Scott. At second, we have Julio Gotay, who played in the majors. At third we've got Joe Foy. Leo Cardenas, who was an All-Star with the Reds, at short. Paul Blair, who played for the Orioles, is in center. Davey May is in right. Plus native players in various positions, plenty of whom were outstanding. And who also liked to win a lot.

Our pitchers were very strong. Juan Pizarro from the White Sox. Jim Hardin and Wally Bunker from the Orioles. And Davey Leonhard, who was my roommate and my best friend on the team. So, even though I'm pitching better, they don't have a roster spot for me.

By the way, the Orioles have cut my pay back—they could do that—from $15,000 to $12,000, but I'm getting $1,000 a month to play winter baseball, which is important since I have a family back in Baltimore. Finally, Hiram Quevas, the club owner, calls me in and tells me they're going to put me on the roster. But they're going to bump Davey Leonhard.

I say, "No, no, you can't do that. He's my best friend. My roommate from A ball in Aberdeen, South Dakota."

And Quevas says, "You worry about you!" And then he gives me a little lecture about life and baseball. "You take care of yourself. Davey's been down here before. I'll take care of Davey."

Then he explained how I was going to get paid. "You get $1,000 a month salary and $350 from the hand of God." He was God. And God paid in cash, in the stands, right in front of everyone, mostly in hundred-dollar bills.

I started to really pitch well. I won my first six games. One game, Elrod tells me I'm throwing so well, that just for fun, he's telling each batter what the next pitch is going to be and they still can't hit it.

And we're in the playoffs. We're down three games to two and I'm supposed to pitch the final game, if there is one. This is where Hiram Quevas makes good on his promise to take care of Davey Leonhard. He puts Davey in to pitch the biggest game of the year, the one that will get us to the final game. And after not pitching for a month, except batting practice, Leonhard pitches a shutout. God is a very powerful guy in Puerto Rico.

So now it's the final game. And we're playing against Santurce's sister city, San Juan. They're side by side, and so are the fans. Divided right down the middle, by maybe one street or an alley or through the middle of a bus. When we play San Juan, you can draw a line in Hiram Bithorn Stadium from behind home plate right across the field, and on the Santurce dugout side you have twelve thousand Santurce fans going totally wild for us to win, and starting exactly one seat away and on the San Juan dugout side you have twelve thousand San Juan fans going totally wild for them to win. They loved baseball. They hated losing. Throwing cups and cans on the field wasn't uncommon. Throwing each other on the field wasn't, either.

Here's the game. Jose Cardinal, a major leaguer from Puerto Rico, playing for San Juan, leads off the game with a home run. The San Juan fans are ecstatic. The Santurce fans are distraught.

I strike out the next eight guys. The Santurce fans are delirious. The San Juan fans are weeping audibly.

Cardinal hits another home run. San Juan rejoices. Santurce wails. We're down 2–0.

In the fourth or fifth, Joe Foy makes an error at third base; I walk a guy; they get a base hit and a line drive to left which hits the fielder in the shin and bounces into center; both runners score and it's 4–0. The runner goes to third and scores on a sacrifice so it's 5–0 and Frank Robinson goes to the bullpen.

It goes downhill from there. Something like 9–2. The San Juan crowd is in heaven. The Santurce crowd . . . well, also headed for the afterlife.

As Davey Leonhard told it from his view from the bullpen, a devoted and depressed Santurce fan decided that San Juan's last rally had done his team in for good. He reached into what seemed to be his lunch bag, took out two pieces of bread, sprinkled something on the bread, and ate it. Davey called it a "rat sandwich." As in, a sandwich *for* a rat. Rat poison on white. They carried him out of the stands . . . staying on the Santurce side all the way because that's the way he would have wanted it.

They take their baseball very seriously down there. It kind of puts your priorities in order. For a minute. And then you think, well, at least my arm still feels good. And I'm going back to the majors.

A Difference of Opinion

I was the target of Earl's temper plenty. But so was the rest of the world. Given a choice, I preferred it when he was mad at anyone but me. No matter who was the victim, afterward he'd always say, "I wasn't mad. I was concentrating too hard." And he believed it.

Like when we're playing a game in Florida and Earl is coaching third base. I'm not pitching, which is just as well because we're getting outpitched.

Of course, Earl isn't giving the credit to the other team's pitcher. He's giving the blame to the umpire. Never mind that from where Earl stands, his view of the plate is a forty-five-degree angle also blocked by the batter's ass. The pitcher pitches; the umpire makes a bad call. That is, a call Earl didn't agree with, but which, coincidentally, the opposing manager thought was a brilliant and sensitive call. That is, a strike.

On the next pitch, the umpire makes another call Earl hates. Another strike. Earl kicks the dirt at third. He spits. (I should note here that, from the bench, I have the same view that Earl has, but under oath, I'd have to say the umpire is calling them like they are, strikes.) One more pitch, and one more call that Earl, really concentrating now, cannot live with. Strike three. He rushes toward the umpire and calls him something that cannot actually occur in nature. The umpire throws Earl out of the game.

Earl picks up third base . . . the actual base . . . and leaves the field. The umpire is shouting and Earl is strutting away, base under his arm like his groceries, heading toward the locker room. We played the rest of the game with a little lime outline of third.

After the game, Earl is in his office talking to himself. He's using the base for a place mat for his dinner. I stick my head in.

"Earl, I didn't know you were that fast."

"What the fuck are you talking about?" he snaps, still pissed off.

"I didn't know you could steal third," I say, and I head for the showers.

Earl paid a fine and returned the base. He was really concentrating hard that day.

Sensitivity Training

Earl Weaver wasn't "nice." He looked out for his players and he cared about the team, but he wasn't nice, not so it showed. He thought the "nicest" thing he could do for everybody was win baseball games.

He was a guy with a job. His job was to win. And this is a guy who measured everything with stats. They even called them the Weaver Stats. He kept track of everything. What batter hit what kind of pitch to which field. Opposing pitchers against us at home versus away. Left-handers. Right-handers. Knuckleballers and sidearmers. How many guys we left on base in July when it was hot and how many in September when it was cool. Hit-and-runs. Slugging averages. Walks. Steals. Opposite field doubles. Stats for everything. ERAs. RBIs. HRs. DPs. But there are no stats for NICEs.

It's not that he got up every morning and said, "How can I be a completely heartless asshole?" It's that he got up every morning and said, "I have to get rid of everything that has nothing to do with winning." It's the game, the game, the game. "I'll be nice in October . . . unless we're in the World Series. Then I'll be nice at Thanksgiving."

I asked Boog Powell once, "What's the nicest thing you ever actually saw Earl Weaver do . . . during the season?"

Boog asks if it has to be during the season and I say yeah.

He thinks for a long time. A real long time. And then he says that once, after a game in the minors in Appleton, Wisconsin, a game they lost bad and needed to win bad, so Earl was mad as hell and replaying every mistake in his head—after this game, a fan comes up to Earl and shoves a piece of paper in front of him and says, "I want your autograph," and he kind of pushes Earl, but not on purpose.

Earl, who's in his own world, sort of shoves the guy away and says, "I don't want to give any autographs."

Well, the guy falls down, and when he did, you could see he has a club foot. Earl looks down and sees this big foot sticking out and reaches down and helps the guy up.

I say, "Boog, did he give him the autograph?"

Boog says, "Oh, hell no. We were in the middle of a race for first."

1969 and '70

The Beginning of Winning. The Beginning of Whining.

You know that expression, "Tomorrow is the first day of the rest of your life"? Mine was the day I went back up to the majors and Weaver was my manager. For the next fifteen years, my career had a constant companion, like an ulcer. Its name was Earl.

Jim Palmer won sixteen games in 1969. It was to be the start of one of the great pitching careers of all time. In August of '69, he threw an 8–0 no-hitter against Oakland. He beat Minnesota 11–2 to clinch the American League pennant.

Nineteen-seventy was even better. He got his fiftieth major league win by beating Cleveland, 3–0. He started his first All-Star game and pitched three shutout innings. And he had Cleveland to thank again when he won his twentieth that year.

Earl Weaver led his Orioles to the American League play-offs against the Twins. Palmer won a 6–1 decision to take the pennant.

In the World Series, against Cincinnati, Earl started Jim in Game 1, and the Orioles won it, 4–3.

Together, Earl Weaver and Jim Palmer and the rest of the Orioles won the 1970 championship.

The Psychology of Managing

When I hurt my arm in 1967, Jim Hardin was a promising, but not-overflowing-with-confidence, pitcher who was called up to the majors to replace me. He went 10–5, and in '68 he ended up 18–13 and at one point was 17–8. But then he got a shoulder injury in Puerto Rico in the winter of '68 and was treated like a sort of a fringe pitcher.

I know the feeling. I lived it. It's like leprosy. "Oh, he *coulda* been good." "He was *almost* good." "Someday, he *might be* okay again." Translation: Don't get near him or you could catch a case of End-of-Career-itis.

So now it's 1970, I've defied the odds and beaten leprosy, and we're in Chicago. It's raining in the second game of a doubleheader and Hardin comes in to relieve. For whatever reason, he's not particularly liked by some of the guys. But Brooks Robinson and Davey Leonhard and me, we think he's a decent guy if you get to know him, which most of the others didn't do.

Hardin really was an impressive pitcher before he hurt his shoulder. He had great control. And he could be good again, if . . . *If* he pitched a couple of games with some runs to back him up. *If* he had good stuff two starts in a row. *If* things that could go either way go his way. *If* pretty much decides careers.

Somewhere along the way, Hardin had learned self-hypnosis and his key word was "jam." I can't remember if it was key because he would get *into* a "jam" or it was something he repeated to get *out of* a "jam" or if it had to do with the fruity stuff you put on toast. He'd get into these self-induced hypnotic trances and then pitch, and if you're a ballplayer you don't knock anything that might, possibly, maybe, who-knows, work. (The stuff about wearing year-old sweaty jockstraps when you're on a winning streak is all true.)

Anyway, the White Sox had just cleaned the bases and

then got two more men on before Hardin came in. So his job is to keep the guys on base (what they now call "inherited runners") from scoring. And that was the thing he didn't do. Actually he didn't know, at this point, that he wasn't going to do it, because there was a rain delay. So there are two men on, if and when we resume the game.

Rain delays are bad for everybody but mostly for pitchers. You think too much. And, if you're on Earl Weaver's team, you get somebody to think for you. Earl. The more it rains, the more you think. And the more Earl thinks. And the more you think about what Earl thinks and you think about what he thinks you think and you just think too much and then the game starts again. An hour later.

And even Cy Young would've lost his concentration. So, Jim Hardin would for sure. Unless maybe he's in one of his "jam" trances.

Now he's going back out to the mound and I've been where he is so I say, "Jim, you got a great fastball tonight, just use it. You're throwing well. You're popping the ball." I'm trying to pump him up, get him back in the game, get him to forget some of the overthink he's been thinking. I was sort of coaching him.

Earl doesn't say a thing, but I think I felt the hot glare of his X-ray eyes burning a small hole in my forehead.

See, Earl doesn't want me or anybody else "coaching." Coaching sends the wrong message. It encourages people. When Earl was a coach in the minor leagues he actually encouraged ballplayers. He said things that were supportive and kind and not mean or cold or heartless . . . so the legend goes. Or maybe people's minds play tricks on them and you just subconsciously want everyone to have at least some characteristics of a regular human . . . even Earl.

Who knows? Maybe Earl Weaver really did once show a shred of feeling for a guy struggling to make his body perform physical feats on command against other guys who want more than anything for him to fail, while huge, loud groups of crude people holler and boo and drink beer. Maybe back then, Earl said, "Hey, don't let it get to you, kid," or "Settle down, you got a whole team behind you," or "One game doesn't matter."

Maybe he did. Back when he was "coaching." But once he got to the majors, he stopped "coaching" and started "managing."

As a big league manager, Earl used a different kind of motivation. Psychologists will tell you, there's Positive Reinforcement and Negative Reinforcement and, in honor of Earl, *Fucking Reinforcement*. "What the fuck are you bitchin' about today, Palmer?!" "Just throw the fuckin' ball across the fuckin' plate, past the fuckin' batter!" "Can't we get a fucking hit against this mother-fucking team?" "Oh, *fuck-fuck-fuck!*"

Back to the game. One hour later. A lot of overthinks later. Hardin goes out there and the first guy hits a double. The next guy homers. It's safe to say, bad start. It gets worse. The next guy doubles. The fourth guy homers. There's a pattern here, and it's not pretty.

Speaking of not pretty, here comes Weaver to take him out.

Hardin walks off the mound, through the dugout, and down into the locker room. It's quiet. It won't last long. Earl stomps over to me like Yosemite Sam. Earl says, I mean, he hollers, "Don't you fucking ever tell him he's got a good fucking fastball! I'll fucking tell him when he's got a good fucking fastball! And he doesn't! Not today!" (At this point, Earl is "managing.")

And I think to myself, when I was pitching, if I told a fielder he didn't do his job, Earl was all over me for getting down on somebody, but if Earl does it, it's "managing." If Earl *doesn't* give somebody encouragement and gives him *discouragement*, it's supposed to motivate the guy? So then, nobody better tell anybody they're a good hitter or good base stealer or good curveball pitcher or good anything, because then they might play shitty. That's how bad Earl wants to win. How bad he has to win. It doesn't make sense but it's all about winning. From the gut, not the head. It's *Fucking Reinforcement*, Earl Weaver–style.

Maybe that's the difference between coaching and managing. Yeah, that must be it.

The Really Supreme Court

Justice was swift and sure in 1969. The charges against you were read; witnesses spoke their piece; you testified; and the judge handed down a verdict. If it seemed unfair, you had the option of appealing and getting absolutely nowhere.

It was the Orioles' kangaroo court. After every win, instead of the players racing for their cars and their homes and their dates, like every other team in the league, we stayed for the postgame trial. Charlie Lau, one of our coaches, rigged a stringy mop to the headpiece of a catcher's mask and created a homemade version of one of those British powdered wigs for our judge, who banged his gavel—a Hillerich & Bradsby Louisville Slugger—on a locker door and turned to face the accused.

Court was in session. Justice Frank Robinson presiding.

Like August 14, 1969, a night I'll never forget. Not just because it's the night I pitched my no-hitter. It's the night I got one of the most cherished awards of my career. The John Mason Baserunning Award. Cy Youngs and Gold Gloves pale by comparison.

But I'm getting ahead of the actual court docket. First the misdemeanors. Justice Robinson fined Eddie Watt for yawning. One dollar. Watt protested. Justice Robinson glared. Watt paid.

Then Don Buford was charged with talking to young

ladies in the stands. Fine: one dollar per lady. Total fine: three dollars. Buford protested. He claimed he talked to five women.

On to the major crimes and punishments. Justice Robinson identified the guilty parties and gave them awards, which the winners (or losers) were required to display in their lockers until the next session of court.

Like the John O'Donoghue Long Ball Award, in honor of the former Indian who had a tendency to throw fat pitches that ended up getting hit so hard they sometimes didn't land in the same county as the baseball park. Fortunately, no winner was declared on August 14.

Or the Chico Salmon No Touch Award to recognize fielding prowess that had all the deftness of a rhinoceros knitting. That night it went to Paul Blair for a ball he caught and then somehow dropped in the third inning. Chico would have been proud.

Blair was a double winner since he got the Weak Swing Award too, for his blazing, multifoot pop-up in the seventh.

I can't remember who got the Don Buford Red Ass Award that night. It was a toilet seat painted red that went to the guy who got the most pissed off the fastest and easiest over the smallest incident. Jim Hardin seemed to win a lot. And, if no one won, it went to Buford where it felt most at home.

And, of course, there was the previously mentioned John Mason Baserunning Award. Blair almost got a hat trick that night by getting put up for his third award, the Mason "Shoe," which is what the award was—an old, rancid, rotting baseball shoe. But Justice Robinson overruled himself and gave it to me.

Naturally, I protested. I had just gotten a no-hitter. What else did they want from me?

According to Robinson, better baserunning. I was thrown out at home trying to score from second on a short pop-up to Reggie Jackson. Our third-base coach, Billy Hunter, sent me home. When I got there, the ball had already been in the catcher's mitt a good half hour or so. I ended up doing a somersault at the plate, which entertained the crowd, bruised my heel, amazed several teammates, but had no effect on my being called out.

We raised eleven dollars that night that went into the kitty that was supposed to pay for a big, end-of-season party but ended up going to charity because the reason we held court wasn't to have a party. It was to win.

Court was in session after every victory. Never after a loss. Earl had come up to manage us in the middle of '68, and by '69 we were healthy and winning. We had the talent. But we needed to make the team into a team. That's what Earl did as a manager. That's what Frank did with the kangaroo court.

We stayed after the game, we laughed, we played hard, we tried harder. One-dollar fines and red toilet seats motivated us and made us a team.

Did it work? Well, we won the World Series the next year.

How to Piss Off a Whole City

The press hates ballplayers when they don't talk or when they just talk in clichés—*"We played good, we played hard, took advantage of their mistakes, I just thank the good Lord for the chance to play, coulda gone either way, great bunch a guys"*—but they love you when you say something worth quoting. The trouble is, ballplayers, me included, sometimes don't know when to shut up. We say something and decide suddenly we must be the next Johnny Carson, and we keep going until we've said something we're going to read about the next day and say, "What kind of asshole said that?" Oh, it was me.

All of which is a setup to my very clever remarks before the All-Star game in 1970, the first All-Star game I'm going to start. They're having the press conference and one of the reporters says to me, "Palmer, your tie looks just like the one that Tom Seaver had on yesterday."

I come back with, "Oh, it was a gift from Tom for us letting him win the World Series last year."

Big laugh from the crowd, which is 90 percent reporters. Hey, I'm not just a pitcher, I'm an *entertainer!* The lights hit the stage. Drumroll. Rim shot. Why stop now? I don't.

"Come to think of it, I bought it in Cleveland. There's not much else to do when you're in Cleveland."

Huge laugh. God, I'm good.

Those reporters loved me. I was quotable. They quoted me. Everywhere. Including Cleveland. So, the next time we were in Cleveland, they greeted me with open . . . fire. They ran a scathing editorial in the *Plain Dealer;* they gave me a record greeting at the ballpark, all boos; and they cheered when we left town.

Just play baseball. Don't try to be Johnny Carson, and he won't try to throw high fastballs.

I Was Right, He Was Wrong. It's That Simple.

People say Earl and I never agreed on anything. And Earl would probably go along with that. So, I wouldn't. But I'd be right. And he wouldn't admit it. I sometimes did agree with Earl on things, just not baseball.

I was logic. He was gut. I would think (some people might say overthink . . . Earl being one of them). He went by feel.

So, in 1970, we're going up against Cincinnati in the World Series. We're going to go on to win the Series and it's going to turn out to be Earl's only world championship. He managed us in the '69, '71, and '79 Series but we lost.

Anyway, nobody knows any of this, even somebody who

thinks as hard as I do, because we haven't even played Game 1 of the '70 Series yet. We're just getting ready. And Earl is wound so tight you could bounce a dime off his temper.

He's conducting one of his infamous pitching meetings, which were to rational thought what Michael Jackson's life is to . . . well, rational thought. That is, complete strangers. So, he's in midorbit, sailing through this meeting, rarely touching earth, getting us worked up for taking on the monstrous Big Red Cincinnati Machine.

Earl is shoveling and the bullshit is knee deep.

Okay, our defense is good, real good. And our pitching is strong. But, all of Earl's fantasies aside, our hitting, in professional terms, ain't shit to theirs, which I'll get to soon enough.

I said our pitching was strong, and it was. I had a good year, 20–10. McNally went something like 20–5, great year. Cuellar tied for the Cy Young Award in '69 and should have won it in '70 but got beaten out by Jim Perry of the Twins. We each throw some good stuff, different stuff. Me, a right-hander, and these two veteran left-handers. Good, right?

Except for one thing. The Big Red Machine was called the Big Red Machine because they were great big guys who got big hits; and they got those big hits in big games; and they wore red; they could make you turn embarrassed-red; they liked to play for your red blood; and they kept coming like a goddamn gigantic fucking, very big, very red, machine. But otherwise, they were no problem.

Incidentally, we were not called the Large Orange anything.

Here comes Earl's rundown of their lineup, which is going to end with Earl's selection of a starting pitcher for the opening game. Remember that, psychologically, the way you start is likely to influence the whole World Series . . . and that it would be ideal to not start by getting your ass handed to you on a big, red platter.

So, here they are:

- Johnny Bench, who's going to the Hall of Fame, a high fastball hitter.
- Pete Rose, who belongs in the Hall of Fame, a high fastball hitter.

A small, illogical fear begins to grow in me.

- Tony Perez, who will probably get to the Hall of Fame, a high fastball hitter.
- Lee May, who in his career will hit 354 home runs on mostly, yup, high fastballs.

My little fear is getting bigger, but I tell myself, no, it's impossible. Forget it.

- Bernie Carbo, Rookie of the Year, who got there on . . . what else? . . . high fastballs.
- Cesar Geronimo, high fastballs. There's a pattern here.
- Bobby Tolan, guess what kind of balls he hits? The high, fast kind.

My fear is fully grown, but even Earl isn't that crazy, is he? He wouldn't . . . would he?

Hey, Cuellar throws screwballs. McNally throws a great curve and a killer of a slider. I throw, in the words of *The Sound of Music,* ". . . a few of their favorite things." High fastballs.

The moment of truth. Silence. Earl speaks. "First game, Palmer starts."

I'm speechless. Okay, I'm never speechless. I say, "Earl, seven out of eight of 'em hit the high fastball."

Pause. Everybody looks at Earl.

He says, "Not *your* high fastball."

With a completely straight face, as if this makes as much sense as gravity keeping his short, little Double A body glued to the earth, he says "not *your* high fastball." And the amazing thing is, he believes himself.

Did I believe him? My head says no. Every correctly connected synapse in my brain says no.

I pitched. We won, 4 to 3. And we won the Series in five games.

I could say Earl was right. I could, but I won't.

1971, '72, and '73
Three More Twenty-Win Seasons. Way to Go, Earl!

I won almost a hundred games from 1970 to '73. It must have been my manager.

For Jim Palmer, winning twenty games a season became almost expected from 1970 onward. He did it every year, for four years running. And Earl Weaver steering the Orioles to the American League playoffs was nearly as automatic during those years.

Jim struck out a career-high thirteen Cleveland batters on July 1, 1971. He pitched in the All-Star game that year. He beat Cleveland for win number twenty. And the Orioles had four pitchers with twenty wins in '71.

Jim went on to beat Oakland, 5–3, in the American League Championship Series. And he beat Pittsburgh, 11–3, in Game 2 of the World Series, though the Pirates went on to win the championship.

In 1972, he was back in the All-Star game, back with another twenty wins by September, and got his one-hundredth win against Milwaukee.

Then came 1973. Along with another twenty-win season, Jim racked up a 2.40 ERA, and he was number two in the MVP voting. To cap it all off, he won his first Cy Young Award.

And on October 6, Earl pitched Palmer against the Oakland A's in Game 1 of the American League playoffs once more. Jim shut them out, 6–0, but the Birds lost the pennant.

The Leonhard Strategy

Davey Leonhard was probably my best friend on the Orioles in all the time I played. He always said he had no business playing in the majors and only did it as a summer job. It was actually sort of true.

Davey had gone to Johns Hopkins University, which definitely made him the one and only big league player to go there. Now it's 1963 and he's teaching school and he's a social worker. It's summer and Davey and his friends always played in some kind of league and got summer jobs to make extra money.

Davey had pitched in high school, was 0 and 2, and in his words, "could never get anybody out." Then he pitched for Hopkins and played a little better, like 3 and 2, but baseball at Hopkins is not at all like playing lacrosse for Hopkins, which is important and/or holy. In other words, they had a crummy record but no one knew it.

But he did have a game or two where he threw pretty well, and this scout named Walter Youse had seen those games.

So Davey goes into this sporting goods store to scrounge up equipment for his summer league guys, and there's Youse, who says why don't you play professional in this league for ex–high school and college guys and get paid to play. Youse knows the guy who owns the store and gets Davey a 20 percent discount on a new pair of spikes. That was sort of his signing bonus. Not even a whole pair of spikes, just 20 percent off.

Well, this is too good to be true because Davey just wants to play and wants somebody else to pay for the equipment. Anyway, in this sort of fairy-tale way, he pitches pretty well in the pro summer league and someone says, why not go to spring training with the Orioles.

Why not? That's in Florida, and the trip is free and Davey gets added to the roster and his meals are paid for even if it is only three dollars a day, and he can still go back and teach school afterward. So what if he's the only guy who gets a library card in every town we visit and if he happens to keep up on who runs Russia and what war we're in?

Davey and I found each other, not because we shared a love of the game, but more because we could talk to each other without spitting a lot. He was there for the experience and enjoying every minute of it. He figured, at any moment they might discover he was this mediocre player from a lacrosse and premed school who was really a teacher and social worker.

The fact was, Davey's education really was uncommon in the big leagues. He used words of more than one syllable, and he knew a pronoun was not a ex-amateur noun and stuff like that.

So, when we were playing in Puerto Rico, the *Baltimore Sun* asked him to write a story about playing down there. Davey decides to key on the overabundance of cockroaches on the island, claiming that the roaches were capable of getting our sandwiches out of the baskets that were kept in the team bus luggage racks, taking them down to the seats and then eating them before we finished playing a game. The natives didn't take kindly to this characterization and referred to him as "Cucaracha Leonhard," but not in a loving way.

Needless to say, when we got up to the majors, Davey's relationship with Earl Weaver was different than mine. First, Earl thought Johns Hopkins ought to learn there's no "s" on the end of John. And second, Davey wasn't always sure Earl knew who Davey was.

In fact, a lot of people didn't know who Davey was sometimes. My ex-wife, Susie, who may not have loved the game with the same passion as say, Yogi Berra, used to bring her knitting and/or a friend, who usually liked baseball even less, to the games. When the Orioles got this new scoreboard, it would say who was in the bullpen, for instance: "McNally

Warming." And her friend, Phylis Cree, looks up and sees "Leonhard Warming" and she says, "The Orioles must have gotten a new player named Leonhard Warming."

But still, Davey Leonhard (a.k.a. Warming) was pitching pretty well there for a stretch. And Earl decides to come up with his Davey Leonhard strategy.

We're in the '71 World Series against the Pirates and they are fearsome. Monstrous. We're watching them. They're watching us. And even in watching, they're scarier than we are. They have big, mean watchers. We just have regular watchers.

But we have the pitching. Four twenty-game winners. Pat Dobson, Dave McNally, Mike Cuellar, and me. I think by now Earl has already pitched McNally once and Dobson once so he's is trying to decide which of us to pitch next, in Pittsburgh. But he goes up to Davey the day before the game and says, "How do you feel?"

Davey says, "Are you talking to me?"

Earl says, "Yeah, how are you feeling?"

Davey, kind of cautiously, says, "Fine, Earl. Why? You've never asked me how I felt before."

Earl says, "I want you to warm up to pitch."

Davey says, *"Me?"* Earl nods. Davey says, "Why?"

Earl leans over and says, "To scare 'em."

Now Davey feels it's his duty to help Earl out here. He says, "Earl, the Pirates have been scouting us just like we've been scouting them. They know better than to get scared by me."

Earl goes, "Not the Pirates. I want to scare Palmer, McNally, and Cuellar into pitching better.

Sometimes even a Hopkins education can't teach you everything.

Anyway, Davey always looked at the whole thing as one long summer job. Just something fun that happened to happen. In fact, when we won the championship and they gave him a choice between the World Series ring and a TV, Davey took the TV. He said he didn't wear rings, but a free TV was too good to pass up.

Not your average jock view of the world.

Rooney, As in Mickey

The hardest I ever laughed was in Fort Lauderdale during spring training in 1973. I think I sustained a laughing injury.

This is a short story. As in, a story about Earl being short.

Doyle Alexander is pitching for us. We're playing the Yankees.

It's the third inning, and the Yankees are up 11–0. The third inning! We have six more to go, and we're on track to be on the "nothing" end of a 33–0 shutout. This is not the part of a baseball game you enjoy.

And, if you play for Earl, you especially don't enjoy it, because he's fuming and he's steaming and he's boiling and he's just generally not being congenial. He thinks somehow, we can have a twelve-run inning and pull ahead if we just "concentrate harder."

The Yankees have this guy, Duke Sims, a left-handed hitter who played against Earl in Elmira, in Double A. He's a second-string catcher behind Thurman Munson. And Sims knows Earl from the days of eighteen-hour bus rides and dust sandwiches. He's seen Earl's veins bulge into 3D road maps before. He knows the real Earl. And he knows how to piss him off.

So Sims, in his chest protector and shin guards, mask pushed back on the top of his forehead, starts walking down the Yankee dugout . . . but he's on his knees, so he's about Earl's size . . . yelling to Earl, "Rooney! Hey, Rooney!" He goes all the way from one end of the dugout to the other, "Rooney! Rooney!"

I look at Sims and I lose it. We all did. Laughing out of

control. Except Earl, who, with every ounce of his all-business, major league manager determination, tries not to look at Sims. He stares down. He looks into left field. He looks into right field. He stares at the ground. He tries the sky. His shoes.

Finally, he can't help it. He looks over at Sims. "Rooney! Rooney!" Earl breaks up. He tries to be serious because he's supposed to. But he can't.

Later I told Earl it was his fault I didn't win another game or two that year because I laughed so hard at Sims I pulled a muscle.

Logic

We were playing the Rangers at Memorial Stadium. A night game. And there was nothing wrong with me that night.

Now there are some people, like sportswriters, managers, coaches, an ex-wife, two children, next-door neighbors, guys at the gas station, tourists from other countries, who would say that was a first for me, not having anything wrong. They'd say there was always something that hurt. My arm or my neck or my elbow or maybe my shoulder or my upper back or, say, my wrist or my forefinger or maybe my lower back or my jaw or my right leg, upper or lower, or my left thigh. But, the truth is, other than those, I never really had a complaint. People exaggerate.

This night, in 1973, I remember clearly, nothing was wrong.

Except I had a fever of 101. I wasn't even sure I was going to go to the ballpark. I'm sweating pretty good, but nothing hurt, so I go to the game.

We're in the locker room and I tell Earl that I have this fever and he says something very sympathetic that I'll never forget. "Jim, you're sitting on my towel."

I go out and I pitch. And I pitch pretty well. Eventually

we score five runs. And a five-run cushion is usually . . . if I'm pitching good . . . it's usually enough for us to win.

I'm sitting there next to Earl, which, in itself, is worthy of press coverage. The only time I sit next to Earl is when I'm pitching and have to be near the pitching coach, who sits at Earl's side of the bench, or when I like Earl, and those two rarely occur in the same phase of the moon. So, it's obviously for the former reason.

And Earl is saying something about everything, yelling and spitting, and cupping his hand around the cigarettes he's not supposed to smoke in the dugout, and thinking up new endings for the word *fuck*. (I really have nothing to complain about. If you're a pitching coach, you have to sit next to him for 162 games and you probably already know all the grammatical forms of *fuck*.)

And Earl looks over at me, knowing I don't feel so good, and knowing we have scored five runs, and he looks me right in the eye and says, "Imagine how sick you would have been if you had stayed home."

And I say, "What?"

So, he repeats it. "Imagine how sick you would have been if you had stayed home."

But I didn't mean "What?" I meant, *What the hell are you talking about and don't you see how twisted your logic is and are you maybe a close relative of Yogi Berra, Casey Stengel, and Norm Crosby?*

Would I have been *sicker* because I stayed home and *didn't pitch?*

Would I have been *sicker* because the Rangers were *destined not to score?*

Would I have been *sicker* because I'd missed out on a five-run cushion, which we were *going to get no matter what?*

Would I have somehow known, being at home, *what would have happened* if I had been at the ballpark, like I had the power to see the future and the past . . . and what am I *doing* even trying to explain this to myself?

And Earl smiles, satisfied that he made his point.

I got a sudden pain, right where I was sitting.

Coincidence

I won my first Cy Young Award in 1973. That's the short version.

Here's the longer version.

The '67 and '68 seasons were sort of like when I was ten years old. In both instances, I wanted to play baseball in the worst way, and I did. I was awful.

I was in the minors and couldn't pitch for '67 and most of '68, and I was in Little League and couldn't hit when I was ten . . . unless you count a .163 average as hitting.

Just when I was ready to give up, both times, things changed. And instead of those times being the beginning of the end, they ended up being the beginning of the beginning.

Nineteen sixty-nine was the real start of my major league career; '65 and '66 were just sneak previews. In '69 I went 16–4, and then, from '70 to '73, had four twenty-win years in a row. And by 1973, my career record was 122–57 and my ERA was down to 2.40.

So what changed? My arm stopped hurting all the time and only hurt sometimes. I had better control. I pitched smarter. I ate pancakes before a lot of wins and got the nickname "Cakes." Our defense was superb. We had a great hitting team. I was even a pitcher who could hit until the DH rule came along and it didn't matter anymore. And I guess that was about it.

Oh yeah, one other small change. Midway through the '68 season, the Orioles moved their first-base coach up to manager. A guy named Earl Weaver.

By the time I came back, in '69, Weaver was in charge. And I do mean in charge, charged up, and charging . . . like a rhino in cleats. I was young. He was my first experience with a maniac.

Earl was a possessed, obsessed, driven man. He drove everyone else. Hard and crazy. His god was "Winning." Every loss was living hell. And living hell was a fair description of living with Earl after a loss.

Earl never pitched, never caught, and wasn't much of a hitter. So he figured he was an expert on pitching. Especially my pitching. He disagreed with me on one out of every two pitches I threw. Maybe two out of two. Maybe more.

He couldn't even *see* the pitches from the bench, so he drove catchers like Elrod Hendricks nuts, giving his pathetic little "ffft-ffft!" Weaver-whistle from the dugout steps to get Elrod's attention and then shout out, "What was the last pitch?"

Elrod would shoot a look over at Earl and say, "Curve-ball."

And then Earl would stomp his foot on the ground and growl, "Oh shit, not a curveball! Why a curveball?!"

That was, until Elrod finally learned to do a perfect imitation of a deaf and dumb guy . . . who happened to be a major league catcher.

Earl insisted I needed to add pitches. He told me that in 1969 and 1970 and 1971 and 1972 and 1973. Every day. He called me in the off-season to tell me.

He'd tell me to throw a curve when I threw a fastball. A change-up when I threw the curve. He'd say it should have been up and in when it was low and away. He'd say they all should have been sliders.

He signaled, gestured, waved, jumped, gyrated, and acted like a hummingbird on speed trying to get me to pitch his way. He'd do entire silent movie scenes from the dugout trying to tell me which pitch to throw and when. He'd send the

Three More Twenty-Win Seasons. Way to Go, Earl!

43

pitching coach to the mound to yell at me, with the exact words, tone, and hot air that he'd used on the poor pitching coach.

And when he decided that wasn't working, Earl would storm out to the mound, in person, or in midget, to be accurate, and scream, "What the fuck pitch are you throwing to this cock-sucking bum?!"

And I'd tell him and then he'd say, "Why the fuck are you fucking throwing that fucking pitch?!" He'd spit and snarl and hiss and buzz and stomp and fume. And then get mad.

We feuded. We fought. I soaked in the whirlpool. He sulked in his office. He used four-letter words in ways I never dreamed anatomically possible. I acted immature. He acted like an infant.

And these were our good years together. We were getting along . . . for us.

And we were winning. Hendricks said, "Earl was much harder on the team when we were winning than when we were losing." So, he was a real son of a bitch!

We won the World Series in 1970 and the American League pennant so often in those years, it was almost monotonous. Earl was on a son-of-a-bitch streak. He was happy because we were winning so he could be miserable to us to make sure we kept winning, which made him happy but he couldn't show it because then maybe we wouldn't win. The son-of-a-bitch school of management.

Okay, under Earl, I won ninety-nine games in five years. Coincidence. Okay, a long, consistent coincidence. And a good coincidence.

For me, it was quite a ways from giving up walks and triples in the Instructional League in 1967 to going 22–9 in 1973. When the Cy Young Award came that year, it was that much sweeter. For one moment, all of Earl's determined, demented, demonic drive to win-win-win, all of the yelling and fighting and arguing, all the "you shoulda throwns" and "why doncha throws" and "what the fucks!" and "Jeezus-H-Kee-rysts!". . . all of it seemed worth it when they said the Cy Young Award was going to a guy named Palmer.

It wasn't just the award. The award I never thought I'd get . . . in 1968 or when I was ten. It was my name on the award.

My father loves to tell the story. It was the Little League banquet in California. When it came time to announce the awards that night, I was going to get three trophies, one for the championship we'd won, one for the batting title, and one for home run leader.

But I wasn't Jim Palmer, I was still Jim Wiesen. My mom had married Max Palmer about a year before and I had kept my name. Until that night. I asked the coaches who handed out the awards to announce me by what I decided was my new name, "James Alvin Palmer."

On his eighty-seventh birthday, Max said, "Through all these years, that night was the highlight of my entire life."

That was the name that went on the Cy Young Award. Palmer. Max loved it. I loved it. Earl loved it. He even said I had the stuff to win thirty games.

Twenty isn't enough! Now he wants thirty! He's never satisfied!

Okay, Earl was a big change. But I'm not giving him all the credit.

When I went from hitting .163 at the age of ten to batting champ at eleven, my dad will tell you that, during a midseason home run drought, he took me out and let me buy a new bat. He'll tell you that I started hitting home runs again after that. So you could assume it was the bat. Just like you could assume it was Earl.

But my dad loves to tell the ending to the story. When he put the new bat away one night next to the old bat, he discovered the bats were identical. It wasn't the bat. It was the aura of the bat.

So maybe it wasn't Earl. Maybe it was the aura of Earl. The sawed-off, pain-in-the-butt, never-let-up, know-it-all, in-your-face aura.

1974 and '75
Lowering My ERA . . .
Earl Ranting Average

In '74 Earl drove me nuts and my arm hurt. In '75 Earl drove me nuts but my arm didn't hurt as much. He wasn't getting any better. I was just getting used to him.

Jim Palmer's arm was sore most of his career. Some seasons he pitched well in spite of it. Some he didn't. In 1974, he had trouble from spring training on. He had begun a regimen of intensive therapy that was to last throughout his major league career. The only treatment that worked consistently was rest.

Despite a tough year for Palmer, Earl Weaver pitched him in Game 3 of the American League playoffs against Oakland. Jim and the Orioles lost to Vida Blue, 1–0.

By 1975, Palmer's arm felt good again. And it showed in his record. Weaver started Jim on Opening Day, and he shut out Detroit, 10–0. By the end of August, he had his twenty wins. By mid-September, he'd earned his 150th major league victory.

And at the end of the season, Jim Palmer won his second Cy Young Award.

Inspirational Words

Earl is supposed to give one those motivational speeches to conventioneers one night after a game in Minneapolis. Now, these speeches are all alike. They're all at conventions that are all alike. Guys who sell stuff . . . cafeteria trays or insulation or dental spit cups. You get introduced by the past grand master of insulation contractors, the Insulator Emeritus, who loves baseball, loves conventions, loves polyester, and loves any country that invented both baseball and insulation . . . or spit cups . . . or cafeteria trays. It doesn't matter. What these guys have in common is they all need to have the fire in their sales bellies relit.

And they believe in athletes. Especially managers. So they're just waiting for the inspirational words of a big league, World Series–winning baseball skipper. And besides, Earl doesn't charge much.

Since it's going to be an after-dinner speech, Earl is going to have dinner first. At this local, uptight, stodgy joint that caters to blue-haired ladies and the above-mentioned traveling "guys who sell stuff." But there are two problems. One, he can't get a table for dinner because he hasn't made a reservation, and two, we lost the game so he's not in a great frame of mind for his speech. And that means he's going to change his frame of mind . . . via vodka transfusion.

Earl and his coaches go to the bar to "analyze the game." Actually, the coaches stare at their swizzle sticks while Earl relives the game, pitch by "shitty pitch" and hit by "goddamn hit."

A couple of us players are at the same restaurant, at the same bar, trying to forget the same game that he's remembering in anal detail. (Of course, we must have been drinking milk. Yeah, milk.)

By the time he's rounding third and heading for his fourth

drink, his face is so red you could pour him in a glass and he'd pass for a giant Bloody Mary. Every time a seat opens up, we slide further down the bar, further from Earl.

Finally, they call his name in the dining room, and Earl navigates his way to the table. Pretty soon, we're also in the dining room, a couple of tables away pretending we don't know him . . . pretending we don't play baseball . . . pretending we're not from America . . . except every once in a while he screams out, "We got screwed by that asshole blind dipshit umpire, didn't we, Palmer?!"

And I glance around like I'm looking for this guy, Palmer.

Earl orders dinner and he's having a drink. He waits for his order and he's having a drink. He eats dinner and he's having a drink. Either (a) he had several more drinks, (b) he had one big drink, or (c) he was drinking very slowly.

And he's still rehashing our loss that day. One inning at a time. One bad call at a time. All bad calls that day. All bad calls, ever. He segues into life's injustices . . . starting with no-good umpires (that would be all of them) and covering every bad trade ever made (all the ones Earl didn't make) and all games he shouldn't have lost (that would be all of them) and all the times he got screwed (which, naturally, would be all games he lost).

His language goes from colorful to off-color to only words that rhyme with *duck*.

And you don't have to be at Earl's table to hear him. In fact, you don't have to be in Minneapolis to hear him. Blue hair is turning bluer. Salesmen are blushing. Women gasp. Men gasp. Then nobody gasps because everyone is silent.

Earl rocks back in his chair, just about to come forward and pound the table for emphasis and a refill. Nature phones in. Earl's gotta relieve himself. Right now. A little too loud, about the volume of a good p.a. system, he bellows, "Where's the toilet?"

A guy at the table behind him says, "The toilet's in your mouth."

Earl rocks forward. Hmm. He's pretty sure that's not the location he was looking for. He makes his way from the table, across the room, and over to the door with the large "M" and little plastic man on it.

While he's in there, he must be thinking, *Maybe, just maybe, I was a touch louder than I should have been. Possibly, my language wasn't quite as delicate as it could have been. Perhaps, I was a vile pig.*

Now, Earl really never meant to hurt anyone. Okay, maybe the players and the coaches and the umpires and most of major league baseball, but no real people. So, he feels bad. He better make amends.

He comes back into the dining room. On his way, he stops at the offended table. Not all of them. That would've taken all night. But at the one where the guy suggested that Earl's mouth only needed a handle in order to flush.

Earl looks at the people at the table with every ounce of sincerity he can muster. His voice is low and discreet. His manner is dignified. He leans over intimately and says, "I'm sorry. You lose a tough one and you can't get a table in the dining room and you have a few drinks and pretty soon the 'cock suckers' and 'mother fuckers' just come out."

Major gasping. All the oxygen is sucked out of the room. Most patrons are also sucked out of the room.

Hey, it was Earl's idea of an apology.

As for Earl's inspirational speech to the salesmen, I wasn't there. I can only assume it was great. The man had a way with words.

Sorry, No Earls

Earl Weaver was a brilliant manager in 1974. He must've been. In September we were eight games behind the Red Sox, and we ended up catching and beating them. Got to be great managing. Calling the right plays. Knowing when to bunt, when to steal, when to go for the hit-and-run.

In fact, it was so shrewd, so clever, so outright ingenious that we even worked on the strategy behind it at a secret meeting. Everyone on the team was there. Except Earl Williams, our catcher, who was visiting family, and, oh yeah, the other Earl. Weaver. His invitation must have been lost in the mail. Or maybe it was "no Earls allowed."

We had a good team in '74. Good pitching, good defense, smart offense. Smart offense, not powerful. We lacked Earl's favorite, not-very-secret weapon, the three-run home run. Play decent ball and hit three-run homers. It's a great plan if you have Boog Powells and Frank Robinsons and Brooks Robinsons. If you don't, if you have promising guys on the way up who may not be able to hit a baseball so hard it disappears, you have to take what you've got and make the most of it.

You start with a secret meeting, which we had at Paul Blair's new house. We had Elrod Hendricks and Al Bumbry and all of our pitchers and, like I said, everyone not named Earl. And we come up with a way to catch the Red Sox: Squeeze every hit and every base and every run you can out of every play. Don't count on, or even dream of, the three-run homers. We came up with our own steal signs and hit-and-run signs and bunt signs and swing and take signs and yield, stop, and no left-turn signs.

If one of the coaches asked us why we didn't follow the regular sign, we'd just say, "Judgment call. I didn't think I could hit that guy so I bunted. Luckily it worked, huh, coach?"

We did the same on defense. Our signs, our plays, our plan. Keep 'em from scoring. Or keep the score low. Pull in. Play deep. Watch the middle.

So the Red Sox get to Baltimore with their eight-game lead. Tim McCarver who just got there from the National League, says later, "I get there with this first-place team, we play four games, and we don't score. Nothing. The second-place team shuts us down. I don't know what to make of this American League."

We won twenty-six out of the next thirty-one. Took it right away from Boston. We finally lost to Oakland in the playoffs.

Of course, Earl would say it's all a bunch of nonsense and we just won it by outplaying them and there were no secret meetings or secret signs. Maybe. But, Earl, how do you explain when you gave the swing-away sign and then Hendricks touched the back of his cap twice, making sure the baserunner saw him, and then bunted instead? Huh?

The One-Inch Strike Zone

He thought he was helping. He really did. He thought he was helping me and the other pitchers on the team, and no matter how much we might have begged him to stop helping us, he kept on helping.

Earl Weaver had convinced himself that accusing, abusing, attacking, and acting like a serial killer with a new machete whenever he was in the presence of umpires . . . on account of their blatant favoritism toward all other teams in professional baseball except the team with little orange-and-black birds on their hats . . . Earl convinced himself that his demented behavior would actually result in the umpires trying harder to do a better, fairer, more Solomon-like job. He really thought verbally urinating on someone could win him over, or motivate him, or get him to reach deep inside for his best effort to help the very one who just peed on him.

This thinking explains two things: one, why Earl was not asked by the United Nations to talk Idi Amin into being a nicer guy, and two, why it never, ever, ever worked with umpires!

Here's one example out of a possible, oh, maybe ten zillion.

Boston. Home of Carl Yastrzemski. He, the Hall of Famer, 452–home run hitter, all-time great left fielder. He, the God of baseball. He, with a capital *H,* who can do no wrong.

No, wait. First a little bit on being an umpire. Little kids dream of being shortstops or quarterbacks, movie stars, astronauts, or, if they're not too bright, goalies. But how many kids think, hey, when I grow up I want a job where everybody hates me? Yeah, I want people to call me names and tell me to perform physical acts (on myself) that double-jointed hookers can't do. Being an umpire isn't high on the fantasy list.

But still, a handful of masochists sign up for 162 days of abuse in exchange for mediocre pay, exotic travel to places like Milwaukee and Detroit, getting to wear twenty pounds of padding and a steel crotch protector in the middle of July in St. Louis, and the opportunity to hang around with baby-faced egomaniacs who chew tobacco and get overpaid for *not* getting a hit two-thirds of the time.

Guys who decide to be umpires have to really love baseball. The very best they can hope for is to only piss off 50 percent of the people. Nobody actually cheers *for* them. And they don't have groupies (except women who are into shin guards). But as bad as they may have had it on their worst day, from projectile beer cans to spit showers to accusations about their mothers' occupations, nothing . . . nothing prepares them for . . . *The Wrath of Weaver.*

Earl Weaver hated umpires with every fiber of his win-or-die being. He yelled at them. He screamed in their faces. He kicked dirt on them. He tore up rule books. He taunted and tortured them. See, Earl had the paranoid feeling that umpires were out to get him. And even paranoids are right sometimes. They *were* out to get him. He had earned it. And all he thought he was doing was helping.

Like that time in Boston. Doyle Alexander was pitching for us and I'm supposed to pitch the next night. Well, the first night Fred Lynn and Yaz and the rest of the Red Sox get a truckload of hits off of us and basically pound us into fine sand.

After the game, one of the sportswriters says to Earl, "Seems like you were having trouble getting Yastrzemski out."

The fuse is lit. Earl is in slow burn. He says, "Whad'ya expect when he gets five strikes!?"

The sportswriter sprinkles a little gas on Earl's fire with, "What exactly do you mean, five strikes?"

Weaver is white-hot. He spews out his theory that goes like this:

> Since the president of the league, Joe Cronin, lives in Boston and goes to the games, the umpires don't want to call Yastrzemski out on strikes because the crowd will boo and hiss and go wild and Cronin will think the umps are doing a lousy job since Yaz is Yaz and the umps will look bad in front of their boss, Cronin, and the whole American League. So, the umps see strike one and call it a ball. And strike two is a ball. And maybe strike three is called strike one. Until basically, Yaz gets five strikes but most of them are called balls. And sooner or later, Yaz finds his pitch and knocks the shit out of it.

At our expense. At least that's Earl's theory.

Being journalistically astute, the *Boston Globe* decides a great way to sell newspapers is to print inflammatory comments from a pissed-off losing baseball manager. So, the next day, there are Weaver's words in great big type, *"It's tough to win in Boston when Yastrzemski gets five strikes."* The other pitchers and I considered buying up every copy of the *Globe* to keep the umpires from reading it.

I cut out the article, and I also cut out this little one-inch-by-one-inch picture of home plate that was printed on the bottom of our pitching charts. I taped the two of them together and put my little arts and crafts project on Earl's desk with a note that said, "This will be the actual size of my strike zone tonight."

He comes in from the field and sees it and comes running out of the office like a madman (that is, like usual) and says, "What the fuck are you talking about?"

I say, "Earl, did you read the article? Everyone else in Boston read the article. The umpires for sure read the article."

He says, "It was a positive article! They're gonna try harder tonight!" *They're gonna try harder tonight?* He meant it. He could have passed a lie detector test. He believed himself. He thought he was helping.

As it turned out, I was wrong about the strike zone. It wasn't like the one I cut out. It was smaller.

Comebacks and Comefroms

I had a great comeback in 1975. The thing is, though, to have a great comeback, you have to have a *comefrom*. Someplace you were, back then, that wasn't great. Something piss-poor, which would be way too kind a description of 1974. Piss-poor was 1974 on my good days.

And, of course, 1974 wouldn't have looked nearly as lousy if 1973 hadn't have been so good. Twenty wins, a low ERA, and my first Cy Young Award. Great stuff.

None of which happened in 1974. The first thing I remember that went wrong was at spring training. It can't start any worse than to start bad right at the start, and it did. I'm taking batting practice, even though this is after the designated hitter rule, and I hit the ball off the end of the bat and I feel this kind of sting in my elbow, in the funny bone part . . . which is the single sickest name for a part of the body, since all it does when you hurt it is feel like somebody with electric teeth took a bite out of your spine, and there's nothing funny about that unless you're Hannibal Lecter.

So, after that, I pitch some games and I don't pitch very

well, but it's early in the year and I don't worry about it too much.

Then one day, I'm keeping the pitching charts, you know, who threw what to who, except I can't hold the pencil very well because my fingers are kind of flipping around on me like a fish who's not too happy about just being caught. I know something is wrong, but like all intelligent athletes I figure maybe it will just cure itself some night magically or when the moon is full or something logical like that.

But I'm not throwing well. I try to hit the outside corner and the ball goes a foot outside. I go for the inside corner and I nearly decapitate a batter I had no intention of brushing back. Basically, I plan to throw the ball to a particular spot and the ball goes anyplace it wants to go. It kind of surprises me each time. But not in a good way.

But Earl sticks with me. He even calls me into his office and says, "I have confidence in you. I don't care how many games you lose, even if you lose twenty games, I'm putting your name in the lineup."

Wow, Earl is being . . . "nice." You have to feel good when somebody stands by you like that and has that kind of faith. I feel better already.

What I don't know at this time is that I've hurt my ulna nerve and all I'm doing is making it worse. I just keep pitching. After all, Earl has confidence. He's keeping me in the rotation, living up to his promise.

I lose my next seven starts.

Earl calls me in his office and says, "Jim, I know I told you I'd stick with you even if you lost twenty games, but I have to be concerned about the whole team and about winning ball games, so I'm putting you on the disabled list."

Okay, so he loses confidence thirteen games short of his promise. It's the thought that counts. And winning.

I go see Dr. Kerlan, who had diagnosed my biceptal tendonitis in 1968. He looks me over, asks me about three questions, and tells me I have "ulna nerve entrapment." He says I have to either rest it for six weeks or have surgery.

I say, "Aren't you even going to examine me?"

And he says, "If it'll make you happy, I'll examine you, but you have ulna nerve entrapment. We can operate and lift the nerve out of the groove where it's irritated and staple it to a safer position." Right away, the idea of stapling my nerve is darn appealing. While we're at it, why don't we drop my right eye in a blender?

Dr. Kerlan says, there's always the alternative of six weeks of rest.

Now, even though Earl doesn't want me pitching right now, six weeks is not what he has in mind. It's about five and half weeks too long. Earl's thinking more like a long weekend.

I remind Dr. Kerlan that we're in a pennant race and that my salary for the next year depends on how I pitch this year. And he reminds me of where the door is. He also mentions that he has seen five thousand pitchers in twenty years. That's the actual count. He's seen more pitchers than Hank Aaron, Roger Maris, and Ted Williams ever saw, combined.

I tell him the Orioles won't believe me, so Dr. Kerlan calls Frank Cashen, the GM, for me and tells him. Cashen and Weaver believe him.

For about three weeks.

I work around the house, left-handed. I play tennis, left-handed. I drink lemonade, left-handed. A lot of lemonade, so I go to the bathroom left-handed. My right hand doesn't do anything. I just sort of take it with me wherever I go. I figure, in six weeks, maybe me and my right arm will be okay.

And the pennant race heats up. Instead of Boston running away with it, the Yankees and the Orioles give them a real run. Weaver and Cashen say they need me, and remind me I make $125,000 to pitch, not to sod my lawn, and that my pay just might go down next year, and that three weeks is a very long time, and get your butt out here!

I go from 2–7 to 7–12 with an ERA of 3.25, which is passable for some guys but not for me. But we win the pennant, which is a whole other story, which I will tell, but I start the season lousy, finish lousy, and fill in the middle with solid lousy.

The good news is, I now have all the ingredients of a *come-from* in order to set the stage for a *comeback*. The next year, '75.

Like George Bamberger said, "You're never a pitcher until you hurt your arm." I guess I'm a pitcher. In fact, by now, I qualify as two or three pitchers.

I start out 1975 tentatively. My ulna nerve is staple-free and my fingers aren't flipping like fish. My tendonitis is only semitender. I pitch just fine. At the halfway point I'm 13–5, which is exactly fine, and my ERA is 2.08, which is better than fine.

At no time does Earl express any undue confidence in me. He doesn't promise to stick with me or not. He doesn't try to act kind or caring or the "n" word; he acts like himself. Grumpy and grouchy and unpleasant to umpires. And he pitches me.

I start to really go. Unfortunately, the team isn't quite as strong as the year before, but they're scoring runs and backing me and helping me win. Plus I have Paul Blair in center, who I said at the time was worth two runs, defensively, every game.

I win twenty-three games, my fifth twenty-win season, get ten shutouts, the first pitcher in double figures in shutouts since Dean Chance in '64, even relieve once and win, and finish with a 2.09 ERA.

And I get the Cy Young Award for a second time.

That made two comebacks. The one in 1969 and this one in 1975. Great years. And I'd trade them both in a minute for the shitty, down-in-the-dumps, comefroms I had to get past. Besides, I never could get used to Earl and "nice" in the same sentence, or dugout.

Who's Crazy?

What does this tell you about me?

Around 1975 the ball club decides it would be a good idea to give pyschological tests to the players. So, to test the tests, they picked two players as lab rats. Me and Bobby Grich.

They figure, if they can learn enough about the two most intense guys on the team to maybe handle us better, maybe get us to be cooperative, so we maybe even do what they say we should do, then these tests are really worth something. And, if not, well, then they just mucked around with our brains and now they can go back to hollering at us and wondering why we won't do anything they tell us.

We take the tests. They ask a lot of questions about taking orders and blind faith and authority figures . . . some of my favorite topics.

For instance, "Is the manager always right?"

Like any good team member who knows who's boss, I say, "No, the manager isn't always right!"

And, "If the manager tells you do something, are you always going to do it?"

I see that word *always* and I answer, "Absolutely not!" because nobody is "always" right.

They have a raft of questions like that, and I have a raft of answers that mostly start with "No."

They conclude that I'm pretty calm and collected under pressure. I maintain self-control under adverse conditions. And . . . I'm completely "uncoachable."

They wanted that military mentality where, if your commanding officer tells you to march straight to burning hell, you say, "Oh boy! Maybe I can get a tan." But I just don't go anywhere or do anything unless it makes sense to me. And I'm sure as hell not following Earl Weaver to hell. Being on earth with him has been close enough.

Turns out, Grich is almost as impossible as me. But not quite. I made him look like Mr. Reasonable. Or, Mr. Less-Butt-Headed.

Unfair. I was not being unreasonable. If they had asked, "Is the manager *ever* right?" I would have said, "It could happen."

For some reason, they never tested the rest of the team.

1976

The Year Everything Changed

**Free agency arrived and suddenly we were
all underpaid. Believe it or not, that was
something Earl and I agreed on.**

*Nineteen seventy-six was the sixth year Jim Palmer won
twenty games. It was the year he won his first Gold Glove.
And it was the year he won his third Cy Young Award.*

*Nineteen seventy-six was also the year ballplayers started
to play out their options. Free agency was on its way in. Few
realized at first how much it was destined to change the eco-
nomics of the game.*

*Earl Weaver was supposed to be part of management. But
he was paid to win ball games. He thought ballplayers who
won games were worth whatever they could get.*

*At the end of the '76 season, when it came time for Jim
Palmer to renegotiate his contract with the owners, Earl took
Palmer's side.*

The Reggie Jackson Era . . . Make That Seven-Eighths of a Season

I would say Reggie Jackson was arrogant. But the word *arrogant* isn't arrogant enough.

If I was accused of *trying* to be perfect, Reggie had no such problem. He was already there. Just ask him.

People in Baltimore thought Earl and I were the odd couple, but that's only because Reggie was just there one season, 1976. If the press liked to make sparks fly between Palmer and Weaver, they'd have had bonfire with Reggie and Earl.

Reggie didn't have managers. He had publicists and business advisers and investors and agents. His agents had agents. Managers could just take their place in line behind all the other guys who made less money than Reggie, hit fewer home runs, didn't get the endorsements he got, and were rarely asked to do talk shows.

I wish he had stayed with the O's. Oh, I wish he had stayed. I would have looked so normal. So low-key and easygoing and cooperative. Earl Weaver's meek, mild best friend.

Reggie was a great ballplayer, almost as great as he thought he was. And he had style. He could carry off the arrogance and the pomposity and the perfection like nobody else. He was Joe Namath without humility.

The Orioles got Reggie and Ken Holtzman in a trade for Mike Torrez, who had won twenty games, and Don Baylor, who was going to go on to be the American League MVP in 1979. Reggie wasn't "Mr. October" yet. That came in '78 and '79. But in '72, '73, and '74, he was already slugging homers and helping win pennants and World Series for the Oakland A's.

And the Orioles only made one mistake. They didn't sign him to a five-year deal. Or even a two-year deal. They let him play out his contract. This wasn't dumb. It was monumentally boneheaded. You don't have to be a front-office wizard or a wealthy team owner to know this. You only have to spend five seconds with Reggie Jackson to know he's not going to stay in Baltimore just because it seems like a swell place to raise a family. He's going where the money is. You got the money? You get Reggie. Otherwise, this is just a stopover on his way to the next bank.

So Hank Peters and Jerry Hoffberger let Reggie come and then let him get away . . . after giving up two great ballplayers. Did I mention how unbelievably idiotic this was? How classically brick-brained? Well, if I haven't covered it already, it was stoop-id, with a capital STOOP.

Anyway, His Reggieness shows up five weeks late, and even though he played pretty well eventually, the whole season was about five weeks late for the Orioles. Five more weeks and we might have won the whole thing.

The first road trip, Earl and the team get our true intro to what Reggie is about. Earl is sitting up front on the plane and here comes Jackson. Earl stops him in the aisle and says, "Reggie, you have to wear a tie when we travel."

Reggie smirks his $25,000-per-tooth smirk and says, "I don't own a tie."

See, the A's didn't wear ties. The A's had mustaches. Guys like Rollie Fingers and Blue Moon Odom and Vida Blue and Catfish Hunter. Come to think of it, they had mustaches *and* they had cool names, so I guess they didn't need ties.

Anyway, Earl says, "No problem," and he hands Reggie this tie that's kind of like the ones you get at a restaurant that requires ties and jackets–you know, those polyester-and-fiberglass blends that don't wrinkle even if you land the space shuttle on them.

Reggie holds this tie out like it's a turd, which it might've been, and puts it on.

Then he makes his way to the back of the plane and his

ever-present audience, the press. Reggie is grumbling to all these panting, scribbling, fawning reporters who are hanging on his every word. He says, "This dress code is ridiculous. I'm wearing my $375 Raphael jacket; I got my $125 Gucci loafers and my coordinated Gucci belt and my $110 gabardine pants; I got my $10,000 gold El Presidente Rolex watch. Are they saying I don't look good?"

Big laughs from the press.

Okay, the next day we go to Chicago and we come out to get on the bus and we have this utility guy named Tony Muser who would back up Lee May at first base, a great guy with a great sense of humor. And Tony gets on the bus and he has price tags hanging off of every single piece of clothing he's wearing.

Tony stands at the front and waits until he's sure everybody, including Reggie, can hear him, and he reads his tags out loud. "I got my $29.95 imitation leather jacket from K mart; I got my $9.95 shoes from Thom McCann; I got my permanent-press rayon shirt from JC Penney; and I got my $19.95 wash-and-wear slacks plus matching belt from Sears. I think I look pretty darn good."

The entire team falls apart laughing. (Except maybe one guy.) Earl is practically on the floor in convulsions.

But I wouldn't say it really fazed Reggie that much. When we were at home, he just cruised around town in his black Porsche turbo Carrera with the "73 MVP" license plates and dropped in on his girlfriend in his penthouse apartment.

When we were on the road, he evaluated each city for its *Reggie Potential*, which I think was a mysterious formula of market-size multiplied by personal exposure opportunities plus team revenues divided by generosity toward superstars.

- "Milwaukee? I don't like beer and I don't like bratwurst. No future there."
- "Cleveland? I don't like playing to an empty ball-

park. But they do have a Federal Reserve Bank so they must have a lot of money."

• "Detroit? Maybe I could do some car ads."

Reggie had this way of being out for Reggie with no apologies and somehow making it seem okay. He'd say to me, "Diamond Jim, when it's all said and done, you'll get your twenty wins and I'll get my thirty dingers." He turned out to be right about himself and I prayed he was right about me. I think his self-confidence hit half of those home runs. It wasn't just cockiness. All right, it was cockiness, but it was his style, too.

Reggie Jackson was the only guy who had the guts to say to Stan Musial, at the Hall of Fame ceremonies, "Stan, I'll be glad to sign any autographs you want after the induction." To Stan Musial! Stan "the Man" Musial! Stan "Lifetime Average of .334" Musial!

Chuck Thompson, the great Oriole broadcaster, once made this Reggie observation. "There isn't enough mustard in the ballpark to cover this hot dog."

But Reggie was an equal-opportunity egotist. He was that way with everyone. With Earl and with the owners and with the front office. "Hey, just pay me, I'm worth it."

For a manager like Earl Weaver, who prided himself on treating twenty-five ballplayers alike, it didn't go down too well. For an owner like Jerry Hoffberger, who liked to say, "Never reach for a deal," Reggie's price was a hell of a reach. And for Hank Peters, who had to make Jerry's ideas seem like his own ideas, it was a bad idea.

You could add Baltimore to Reggie's evaluations.

• "Baltimore? Next."

To him, that wasn't a put-down. It was what he believed. And Reggie was nothing if not sincere.

He'd put his hand over his heart, in what we called his Napoleon pose, and he'd be sincere. Even if he was standing in nothing but his jockstrap, like the time at the meeting with the player representative when he said, "You guys gotta take care of yourselves because I'm gonna be all right. I'm gonna get my money." And everybody nods.

And he got his money. But not in Baltimore. They let him get away.

You've got to be cool and you've got to be good to stand there in your jock, with your hand over your heart, and tell everybody else how rich you're going to be.

Of course, it was an Oscar de la Renta jockstrap: $65.

The Code

There's a sort of unwritten code in baseball, like the code of the Old West. *Sometimes you gotta do the right thing even when it seems like the wrong thing on account of you're doing it for your team.* It's unwritten because (1) if you wrote it down, you'd realize it makes no sense, and (2) everybody in the game already knows what it means. It's a man thing. A macho thing. A male-man-macho-testosterone-gonad-phallic thing!

It's the Code of the Game, which is not to be confused with the rules of the game, because in order to be *in* the Code something has to be *against* the rules, not to mention against the law in most states. The rules are for rational people. The Code is for guys. There's a clear difference. You gotta do it or you're a pussy.

So, Dock Ellis of the Yankees threw a pitch too close to one of *our guys* in a game in '76. (This is the same Dock Ellis who claimed to have pitched while on acid or marijuana or something mind-waltzing, but not on this particular occasion.) Reggie Jackson . . . who was barely one of *our team* since he had just joined us that season and, as I said, five weeks late since he had been holding out for money . . . Reggie Jackson said to Dock Ellis, "If you're gonna throw at somebody, throw at me!"

Now, Code or no Code, that comment would *not* somehow make it okay for Ellis to throw the ball at Reggie. No. It was dugout-taunting and baiting and childish I-dare-you stuff. But it didn't warrant Code retaliation.

But Ellis did it. When Reggie came up to bat, Ellis threw right at him, the Code-ignorant fool! (They ought to have a Code test before you can play baseball, like the SATs, only with cheating allowed, of course.) Ellis hit Reggie square in the cheek with a hard one. Reggie went down just as hard, and they took him on a stretcher to Union Memorial Hospital.

That's when I knew. Earl knew. And I knew Earl knew that I knew. A Code moment.

Earl Weaver never, ever told me or any other pitcher to throw the ball at another player. Ever. In fact, he once went ape-shit all over Grant Jackson, who was a left-handed relief pitcher we got from the Phillies. In the National League everybody threw at everybody, especially somebody who was hitting good. We were playing Boston and I can't remember who was up, maybe Carl Yastrzemski, and Grant fires one right at Carl's head. Weaver is out to the mound in a blur.

Earl says, "Grant, who's playing third for us?"

Grant stares down like a little kid and says, "Uh, Brooks Robinson?"

Earl says, "Right. You see anybody on their team as good as Brooks?"

Grant stares down again and says, "No."

Earl goes on, "Who's playing first for us?"

Grant mumbles, "Boog Powell."

Earl says, "Anybody close to Boog on their team?"

Grant mutters, "No."

Earl goes through the whole lineup. Grant acknowledges we have great players all around. Earl patiently explains, "If you throw at them, they're gonna throw at us. Our team is better. We don't want to get anybody hurt, do we?"

Grant mumbles, "No, we don't."

Earl screams, full-tilt, *"So cut this shit out!"*

Earl did not say to me, "Hit somebody." First of all it's against the rules. Second, Earl wouldn't do that. He just shook his head and said, real low and slow like Clint Eastwood, *"We can't let that happen."* Now that's Code talk. *"We can't let that happen."* I'm pretty sure the *Dirty Harry* theme music was playing in the background. (Earl might've also said, "Go ahead, make my day.")

It's 4–0. I've got a shutout going over the Yankees. I really wanted to keep that shutout. But I had the Code to uphold. The first guy up was Elrod Hendricks. He'd been a catcher for the Orioles. He played on our World Series team in 1970. He caught my no-hitter in the Puerto Rican League. He caught my no-hitter in the majors in 1969 against the Oakland A's. You can't throw the ball at one of the good guys. That's known Code stuff. I pitch to him and he flies out to deep right center for the first out.

The next guy up is Mickey Rivers, who looks a little like Jiminy Cricket, which is no reason to throw at him, but I don't know him personally and he's on the Yankees and so is Dock Ellis, and therefore Mickey is the unlucky winner/loser of the human-target lottery.

The temperature is ninety-five and I've thrown about 140 pitches so I'm a little tired. I want my shutout, but I've got a job to do. So I throw the ball kinda, sorta at Mickey, and like one of those big-game animals in the Safari Hunter arcade game, he feints and ducks and I miss him. Same thing on the next pitch. I don't want to walk this guy on four balls that *almost* hit him. I mean if you're going to do something wrong, you better do it wrong, right? So, I bear down and I manage to graze him in the upper back.

Roy White is up next, a switch hitter who's batting left, and to take away the first-base hole, we move our first baseman, Lee May, to play behind the base runner, Mickey "The Target" Rivers, who proceeds to steal second on the first pitch. White hits a blooper; Rivers scores; and the shutout is gone.

But . . . we win, 4–1, and the Code lives.

In the meantime, for months Earl has been waging his own one-man crusade against the umpires of the American League, especially Ron Luciano. He and Luciano have escalated to near–global nuclear warfare, and Luciano has just pushed Earl's ballistic button with his infamous comment that he doesn't care who's going to win the pennant as long as it's "anybody but Baltimore."

So the league temporarily replaces Luciano on his crew with Dale Ford in an upcoming series just so Luciano and Weaver won't be on the same field . . . or in the same city. And Earl is convinced that since umpires stick together, this crew will be even more against him and the Orioles than ever because they had to replace Luciano and therefore, *this is wrong.* It may be within the rules, but it's wrong, wrong, wrong! They're going to screw Earl and his team. He's going to have to screw them back. In self-defense, of course. It's a clear Code incident waiting to happen.

So what actually occurred in the game to cause Earl to go totally and absolutely mad-dog incoherently berserk at this crew? What was the heinous deed? The unspeakable transgression? The vile, unforgivable crime? Hey, it's hard to remember. Maybe it was Lee May getting called out on a bad pitch and then getting thrown out himself for overprotesting the call. Yeah, yeah, that's as good as anything to blame it on. It *was* a bad call . . . probably. Awful. Way outside . . . or really low . . . or was it way inside and really high? Anyway, it was a ball, not a strike, and it was a lousy, unfair, mean call by prejudiced umpires out to persecute Earl and his team. Anybody could see that.

The Year Everything Changed   **69**

So Earl storms out onto the field and engages in debate with the officials. The kind of debate where you talk with your hands a lot. And your hands, or rather Earl's hands, to emphasize his points, are flailing around like ninja swords. And one of his fingers of one of his hands that is attached to one of his arms which is being propelled by his little rotary-engine body *might* have happened to barely, just barely, hardly at all, brush the protruding lip of Dale Ford. It was a brush. Not even a tap. A mere brush. Like the feeling of air whooshing past. *Brrr-usssh*. And a justifiable air-whooshing brush. After all, the Orioles were getting screwed.

Out! Ejected! Earl joins Lee May in exile. Thrown out. See? The umpires *were* against us! See? That's why Earl did what he had to do, Code-wise.

Now we're in Detroit and Lee MacPhail, president of the American League, official keeper of the rules and unofficial sheriff of the Code, nails me and Earl on each of our transgressions.

The headline in the *Baltimore Sun* the next day read, PALMER FINED, WEAVER SUSPENDED. A double play.

On mine, MacPhail says, ". . . Palmer was so honest that he would not deny that he hit somebody. He was directly quoted that he threw at Rivers."

I asked MacPhail why he didn't do anything to Ellis, and he said, "Ellis denies that he hit Jackson on purpose. . . ."

Yeah, I was honest and out $500, and Ellis bullshited and held onto his money. Oh, well.

As for Earl, he was banned from the dugout, the clubhouse, the runway, and the press box for three days, according to MacPhail, for "conflicts on the field with American League umpires, and for physical contact with umpire Ford."

MacPhail quoted Ford, who "reported that Weaver hit him in the lips with the knuckles of two fingers and cut his lips." Okay, so much for the mere *brrr-usssh* theory.

Weaver offered a nonapologetic, semiadmission, "I don't deny that my fingers hit Ford. But it wasn't intentional. I was trying to make a point, and don't know whether I was too close or got bumped. . . . I think that I am being treated unfairly. They have thrown me out five times this year and fined me once."

Earl saw them throwing him out as *proof* that he was getting screwed. It was like evidence. That's why he *had* to fight with the umpires. They started it. He'd finish it. Even if he had to listen to the next three games on his car radio.

He felt the same way about what happened to me. "We wind up with a star ballplayer [Reggie Jackson] hurt and out of the lineup for three days and Jim Palmer gets fined by the league. There is no justice sometimes."

There's no justice. But there is the Code.

So it cost me $500 and got Earl booted out of those three games. In fact, the Code got him tossed from a major league record of ninety-one games. A half a season!

I'm going to explain it one more time. *You gotta do what you gotta do for your team . . . even if it's really dumb.* That's how the Code works. Do you get it now?

Door Number Three

Nineteen seventy-six was a screwy year. We had this great team as far as individual talent, but you just knew it was temporary. We had Reggie Jackson, but he's really there just playing out his option so he can become a free agent and go someplace else for a fortune. (Like I said, he actually ranked every major league city on its ability to part with money on his behalf.) The Orioles knew they had to sign him to keep him, but they were living in this dream world of the past so they offered him what would have been a lot of money one year before . . . which might as well have been a century before, salary-wise.

So Reggie holds out and doesn't get back in the groove until much later. And Bobby Grich is also playing out his option for free-agent big money. Which he was also going to get someplace else, not Baltimore.

Money is what's on everybody's mind. I mean somehow everyone knew, without anybody announcing it, that this was the beginning of a whole different era for baseball players' salaries. Like there was the Ice Age and the Iron Age and now we were entering the Pay-Me-Big-or-I'm-Outta-Here Age.

I was having a good year in '76 and money might have been on my mind, too, since it turned out later that I was going to get into a long, nasty stare-down with management types who were longing for the good old days of one year before.

About now we're coming into September and I'd like another shot at Cy and his award. This is the time of the season when the roster can go from twenty-five up to forty, either to help you if you're in a pennant race or keep somebody else out of the pennant race. But nobody really knows if these other fifteen players are any good since they're pretty much untested. So we've got all kinds of guys on the team, a lot from Triple A and from other teams and from rest homes and Little Leagues.

I pitch this game around the twentieth of September and I've got what I called the "Z" lineup, as in, if you have from A to Z, this is your last choice. I have good guys like Dempsey and Singleton and Grich mixed in with What's His Name and No One and Has Been and Pray For Me. About eleven errors later, the game ends and we lose 5–2.

After the game, I say to Earl, "Thanks for the Z lineup. After pitching three hundred innings, I thought I deserved better."

He says, "What the fuck are you talking about?"

I say, "You know, all the walking wounded who you sent out there today to see if it was possible to win in spite of. . . ."

He says, "If you think you're so fucking smart, you fill out the lineup next time you pitch."

I say, "Okay, I will."

And he says, "Okay, you do that!"

And I say, "All right, fine!"

And he says, "Yeah!" And eventually our adult conversation ended probably because the maintenance people had to go home.

I'm supposed to pitch Game 1 of a doubleheader in Yankee Stadium, one of those end-of-the-season-make-up-for-rainouts doubleheaders. I say to Earl, "Okay, I'm gonna make out my lineup."

And he says, "No, you pick one of mine. I'll give you three to pick from." He holds out three lineups. Now, this wasn't the deal, but then even picking one out of three isn't usually up to me since I'm not the manager, so I take the three and check them out.

I'm looking basically for one thing. Center field. We've got Paul Blair, who I personally think can field anything. But ever since he got hit by a pitch, he isn't the hitter he was. But I still think he catches everything and makes up for it. But Earl is platooning Al Bumbry with Blair and he wants Bumbry in the lineup. But I want Blair.

But Earl doesn't.

But I do.

Then I take lineup number one. I don't even look at the batting order. Bumbry in center, no Blair. I wad it up and toss it in the basket.

Lineup two. Bumbry in center, no Blair. Wad . . . two points.

Only one lineup left. I'm hoping it has what I want, which is anybody at any position as long as Blair is in center. Bingo! I take what's behind door number three.

Blair is batting eighth. Reggie isn't playing because of a

bad back. We win 2–0. Blair runs down twelve fly balls in center field, doing everything I knew he'd do. He even gets two RBIs on a single which Earl refuses to remember.

Always the gracious winner, I say, "See? See? See what happens when you let Blair play and let me do the lineup?"

Earl says, "You didn't make up the lineup. I did."

I say, "Yeah, but I picked it!"

And Earl says, "But I made it! I made up all three of them."

I say, "Yeah, how come you wouldn't let me do it?"

Earl says, "'Cause if you made up the lineup and we won, then people would know you're smarter than me."

He smiles and walks away. I smile and walk away. I'm smarter than he is.

Except he figured it all out ahead of me.

Management Has a Heart. A Little, Tiny, Microscopic, Withered Heart.

There's no question, you get overpaid in sports. My only bitch was that I wasn't overpaid as much as other guys were overpaid.

Even Earl thought so. Of course, he thought he got screwed even worse. And I'd agree with him on that one. The guy wins 109 games, 108 games, and 101 games. But they had him working on one-year contracts, every single season, so his life was hanging in the balance in the bottom of the ninth, every game. Come to think of it, that explains him being insane. Why didn't I think of this sooner?

But enough about Earl's problems and back to mine. It's the end of the 1976 season and I'm between the first and second years of a three-year contract. I have no gripes about this contract. Well, I have plenty of gripes about it, but they're not as big as the gripes I'm about to have. The Orioles, specifically, the man who gave Scrooge on-the-job training, Hank Peters, comes to me to renegotiate . . . before my contract runs out.

I had won twenty games in '70, '71, '72, and '73, and came back after injuries in '74 to win twenty in '75 and '76. And I won the Cy Young Award in '73, '75, and '76. The Orioles want to get me to resign before my contract runs out, before I become a free agent, before I put a gun—loaded with a ninety-eight-mile-an-hour fastball—to their heads, before I ask for the moon in small bills, or else I'll go shopping for a team that'll pay me obscenely and act like they want to.

So Hank Peters opens with this speech that's a twisted concoction of compliments and terror. "You're a great pitcher but you could turn to shit tomorrow" (or words to that effect). Like every ballplayer doesn't already worry about that. "With a fastball like yours, Jim, who knows when your arm will go." Thanks, Hank. "What a run you've had, Jimmy. Maybe it's over."

He offers me a $15,000 raise, from $185,000 to $200,000 in the second year, and $215,000 in the third. In case you think maybe that was a lot back then, consider that they were throwing $2 million at Reggie Jackson for five years . . . and it wasn't enough.

I was stunned. I was also naive. I had the misguided idea that after eleven years, loyalty and dedication were worth something. Maybe in a watchdog, not in a ballplayer. What you *did* in the past is just a story to be told over drinks. It's worth nothing. What you can convince them you *can still do* is all that matters.

As mad as I've ever been at Earl . . . and I've been so mad I forgot about seven out of ten ailments I was suffering from at the time . . . as mad as I've been with him, I never felt the way I did about the team management when Peters came in with that horseshit offer. I told Earl, and he took my side. Remember, his life depended on only one thing, winning. He wanted his players paid well to do whatever it took to keep him in black cleats and a Birds uniform.

I told Peters to get realistic. He didn't like that. I didn't much give a shit what he liked. I told him they were out of line.

He stuck to his offer.

I figured we should pack for a move. Finally, I just walked out of the talks.

I couldn't stand to deal to them anymore, so I sent in a lawyer. After back and forth and push and pull and all kinds of posturing and protesting, they went up to $260,000. I wanted $275,000. We were, ironically, back to arguing about $15,000. They agreed to it . . . sort of. Peters said they'd give me a $15,000 bonus if I made a "significant contribution" to the team. That's convincing them of what you *can still do*.

Who knew that their definition of a "significant contribution" wouldn't be satisfied by a 20–11 record, a 2.91 earned run average, a tie for the league lead in wins, starts, and complete games, the Gold Glove for fielding, and second place in the Cy Young voting? I forgot to bat cleanup, steal sixty bases, and stick a broom up my butt to sweep out the dugout.

Peters actually had the guts to refuse to pay. He had promised me that if I had an exceptional year for a major league starter, I'd qualify. Then, at the end of the '77 season, he rewrote his memory to claim he'd said, "you have to have an *exceptional year for you*." Great!

I guess the fact that I had already won the Cy Young Award three times actually hurt me when I finished second. Evidently, the fact that I'd had all those other twenty-win seasons made another twenty-win season run-of-the-mill, not exceptional. In the world according to Peters, only a mediocre player who miraculously gets good earns a bonus. I hadn't been crappy enough in the past!

If anybody was ever looking for a way to drive Earl and me together, they found it. He went to Peters for me. He said he'd rather have me on the Orioles driving him nuts than somewhere else, still driving him nuts . . . or Earl-ese to that effect.

And the Major League Players Association went to Peters. They filed a grievance on my behalf and on behalf of Ken Singleton and Mike Flanagan who were also in line to get the patented Hank Peters *exceptional-but-not-exceptional-for-you*, postseason financial mugging. Singleton batted .328, had twenty-four home runs, ninety-nine RBIs, and was second in the MVP voting. Flanagan went 15–10 with a 3.64 ERA. (Sorry guys, not exceptional. Great, but not exceptional.)

The Players Association wanted to go to arbitration. If they did, there was a good chance we'd all be declared free agents. Earl was back in there, leaping on desks, throwing notebooks, glaring, making his neck vein do tricks . . . all the stuff major league managers do to be persuasive.

Peters folded.

Earl told me later that my contract wasn't the owner's fault, or the GM's fault, or Earl's fault. It was mine. I had signed a crummy contract. He stopped me cold. The guy was right.

Then he went in and signed another one-season deal.

1977

We're Getting to Be Friends, Sort of, Sometimes, a Little

Earl and I disagreed so much, we started thinking it was normal. We fought all week and then, on off-days, played golf in the WGA, the Weaver Golf Association, guys who disagreed with Earl but liked to play golf. It was a big group.

The Orioles and Weaver always seemed to be in the race, and Jim Palmer always seemed to have an equally good record on the mound.

Nineteen seventy-seven was no exception. Jim won his 182nd game to break Dave McNally's Oriole win record. He started the All-Star game. He beat Detroit, 3–2, in eleven innings for his twentieth win. And he won his second Gold Glove.

And throughout it all, Earl Weaver and Jim Palmer argued on the field and off. They sparred privately and in the press on such a regular basis that sportswriters around the country came to rely on them for material. They became as famous for their battles as they were for their victories.

Mind Games, Urinals, and Confidence

Mike Flanagan's head was talking to him a lot in 1977. (Earl Weaver wasn't talking to him, but I'll get to that.) Flanagan's head was having regular conversations with the rest of Flanagan's body. And that's not good. Especially if you're a pitcher.

It's like this. Even though you *throw* with your arm, you don't *pitch* with your arm. You pitch with your head. (Take it from a guy who's in the Sore Arm *and* Head Hall of Fame.)

When your arm hurts, you can soak it, ice it, whirlpool it, X-ray it, MRI it, massage it, tape it, brace it, exercise it, rest it, salve it, balm it, acupuncture it, cortisone it, talk to it, beg it, or cast a spell over it. It hurts, which is why you can't pitch. Therefore, if it didn't hurt, you *could* pitch. Simple.

If your head gets screwed up, it's also simple. You're screwed. You can't soak it or rest it or tape it or acupuncture it. (You could cut it off, but that's drastic.) Your head keeps telling you, in this echoey head-voice: *"You're missssssing the corners, you're loooosing your breaking ball, you're aiming tooooo much, you're not aiming eeeeeenough, you're not con-cen-tra-ting, you're no goooood, you never were any good, everybody knoooows you're noooo good."*

That's the kind of stuff Flanagan's head was saying to him in 1977. It was Mike's first year with the Orioles, and he and I used to sit together a lot on the flights from city to city, the two of us kind of spread out across three bulkhead seats. Mike would have a couple of beers and start talking/moaning/worrying about how he was doing, which wasn't too good since he was 3–8 at the time. I'd listen to young guys like Flanagan and Scotty McGregor and Dennis Martinez because by then I was sort of the veteran, man of experience, old pro, old fart, leader . . . take your pick.

Flanagan is telling me that obviously Earl doesn't have

any faith in him. He figures, how could he have any faith since Flanagan is 3–8? And Earl has never said anything to him about what kind of 3–8 he was having. Like if it was a good 3–8 or a bad 3–8 and there is a difference depending on a lot of things, starting with whether your team is getting any runs behind you or whether they're fielding the ball or making smart plays or at least showing up . . . stuff like that. Plus Mike has just come off spending a year in Triple A under Joe Altobelli who's very compassionate and sensitive compared to most managers. And now he's got Earl Weaver, who isn't all that compassionate and sensitive even compared to most chain gang wardens.

So it's no wonder Flanagan's head has been talking to him and that he's talking to me and that I can hear his head-voice coming through loud and clear. To make matters worse for his head, we're on our way to Boston. Fenway Park is a great place to watch a baseball game unless you're a pitcher, which is what Mike was going to be in the next couple of days. Batters have a habit of hitting a lot of home runs over the short outfield walls in Fenway Park, and the Red Sox pitchers who pitch there half of every season know how to handle it better than visiting pitchers, like Mike was about to be. Visiting pitchers just see pitching at Fenway as a chance for the Red Sox to paint a bulls-eye on your butt and kick the shit out of you. *"You're no goooood, you never were any good, everybody knoooows you're noooo good. . . ."*

Mike's head won't shut up. I've been there. And I've been with Mr. Compassion, the Earl of Sensitivity.

The next day, we're in the visitors' locker room at Fenway. Some architect with a sense of humor has put the manager's office opposite the urinal, or vice versa, depending on which one you think has more status. Well, nature calls and I go to use the facility and right next to me—and a couple of feet below—is Earl. (I'm urinating and Earl is taking a piss.)

I decide this would be a perfect time to talk to him about Mike. Earl can't leave in midstream, or if he does he's going to get his shoes all wet.

I say, "Earl, I sit with Mike on the plane a lot and you know, he thinks you don't have any confidence in him."

And Earl gets, well, literally *"pissed off."* That is, he starts shouting, and I swear, that noise that pee makes when it hits the water actually stops while he shouts and then starts up again when he's finished, kind of like dramatic pauses. He says, during a pee-silence, "Have you looked at his fucking record?! He's three and fucking eight!"

Pee resumes.

"But Earl . . ." I say.

Earl keeps shouting and stops peeing. "Do I have any fucking confidence in him? I put his name in the fucking lineup every fourth day. He ought to fucking know that I have confidence in him or I wouldn't fucking do that!"

Pee resumes.

I finally get my turn and say, "But Earl, the way Mike sees it, he doesn't know how you feel. You know, you can be 3–8 and be good or be 3–8 and be shitty. He hasn't gotten much offensive backup from the team. He played for Altobelli and Joe has a different style than you." (This is called understatement.) "Anyway, if you're going to pitch him every fourth day, it's probably because you think he has a good future but he doesn't know you think that. Maybe you should talk to him."

Pee stops.

I get ready for Earl to shout again, but he doesn't. He's just finally done peeing. He doesn't answer me. He just walks away.

Now it's three days later and we're on the plane out of Boston and, as I recall, Mike pitched okay there.

We take our usual seats and he starts talking. "You know what? Earl came to talk to me."

You can practically cover up the face and the number and still know by the high leg kick that this could only be Jim Palmer, winding up to deliver a fastball.

(Top) Young Jim and his adoptive mother, Polly Kiger Wiesen. At the time, the family lived in New York City and Jim was learning to play catch in Central Park.

(Bottom) Jim Palmer's team photo in the Beverly Hills, California, Little League, 1958. Jim (top row, third from right) is already standing a head taller than some of his teammates.

At age twelve, Jim strikes his pitching pose for the Beverly Hills Yankees in their championship year. He's wearing high-top sneakers because his feet are already too big for the rubber cleats made for kids.

Jim Palmer was a three-letter man at Scottsdale High School. Here's Jim in his junior year, when he was named an All-State end.

Scottsdale High teammate Butch Riggs tests Jim's pitching arm prior to the Arizona State Baseball Tournament in 1961.

Jim's first love in sports was a toss-up between baseball and basketball. Here he is in the Scottsdale High School varsity team photo. Jim (top row, fourth from left), was named to the All-State teams in both his junior and senior years.

(Top) Jim winds up, kicks, and pitches in Winner, South Dakota, in the summer of 1963. He was the only high school player to take part in the summer college league.

(Bottom) Jim (top row, sixth from right), age nineteen, poses with the 1964 Class A Northern League championship team. The manager was a guy named Cal Ripken Sr.

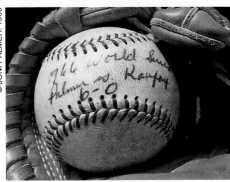

(Top) It's 1966, Jim Palmer's first year as a major league starting pitcher. His career took off fast, as Jim led the Baltimore Orioles in victories with a 15–10 record.

(Bottom) Here's the game ball from Jim Palmer's first World Series start, a 6–0 win over the Los Angeles Dodgers and Sandy Koufax. Jim was the youngest pitcher to throw a World Series shutout, in what was the last game Koufax pitched.

Earl Weaver in a familiar dugout pose, either (a) yawning, (b) gently re-
minding the O's pitcher how quickly he could find himself back in Triple
A, or (c) calling the umpire an illegitimate relative of a bull mastiff.

Three views of the distinctive Palmer delivery, taken at Baltimore's Memorial Stadium (top left and bottom) and in Miami during spring training (top right).

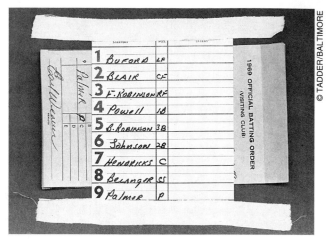

The Orioles lineup was the subject of an occasional dispute between Jim and Earl, but it worked well enough to win six division titles, four league pennants, and a World Series during their years together.

Something seldom seen: Earl and Jim together in the dugout, and neither one hollering. This is spring training in Miami, 1980.

(Right) Earl Weaver calls for a reliever from the top of the mound. Note that with a pile of dirt under his feet, he's almost as tall as Jim.

(Below) Hands on hips: Weaver body language for "Palmer is pitching, there are men on first and third, my hair's getting grayer by the minute, and they won't even let me smoke in the dugout."

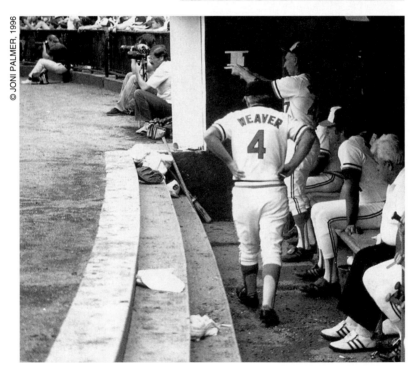

Earl Weaver with his jersey at his induction into the Orioles Hall of Fame. The jersey has just been retired after a decade and a half of turning its back on umpires who have thrown it out of games.

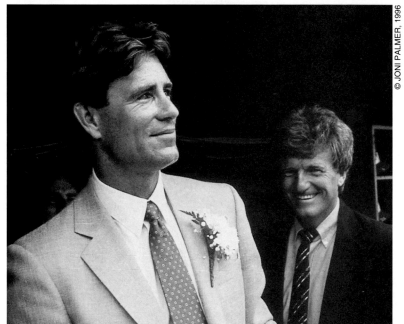

Davey Leonhard, Jim's first roommate in pro baseball and all-time best friend, is on hand to celebrate Jim Palmer Day at Memorial Stadium in Baltimore.

The fans came out to say good-bye to Number 22 on Jim Palmer Day. Signs and banners professed their love and thanks. And Jim couldn't hold back the tears.

You know you've arrived when they put you on a Wheaties box. Commemorating Jim Palmer's induction into the Baseball Hall of Fame in 1990, the eight-time twenty-game winner was on grocery shelves and breakfast tables across America.

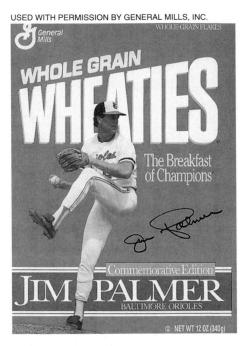

Nobody has become more famous in his underwear than Jim Palmer. His ads made him virtually synonymous with Jockey. This poster sold out nationwide, with Jim giving all the proceeds to cystic fibrosis.

Jim and his extended family stand beside his bronze
plaque at the Hall of Fame ceremony in 1990. From left:
Jim's daughter Jamie; Max Palmer, Jim's second adoptive
father; Ada, Max's second wife; P.J. Pearlstone, Jim's
stepson; Jim; his wife Joni; and his daughter Kelly.

Two Hall of Famers broadcasting
for the O's. Brooks Robinson, the
all-time great third baseman, and
Jim Palmer doing a game in 1990.

Jim Palmer and Joe Morgan at a
press conference the morning after
being selected 1990's Hall of Fame
inductees. They were the twentieth
and twenty-first players voted in
on the first ballot.

Why are these two guys smiling? They've just done what they always did best, win a baseball game. It's the 1993 All-Star Upper Deck Heroes Game in Baltimore's new Oriole Park at Camden Yards. Jim pitched the first inning. Earl was the manager. Just like old times.

I say, "Oh, really?"

He says, "Yeah, he called me into his office. You know, at Fenway, across from the urinal."

I say, "Yeah, I know."

He says, "Earl told me he has confidence in me and I'm pitching better than my record and that's why he's putting me in the rotation every fourth day."

And I say, "No kidding?"

And I listen real close and for the first time in a long time I don't hear his other voice, the echoey one from his head, the one that won't let you pitch no matter how good your arm feels. Not a word.

Mike goes from 3–8 to 15–10. I'm not taking the credit. That belongs to Flanagan. And to Earl. And the architect who put the urinal across from the manager's office.

Fungus

The thing about jock itch is, even when it's not there, it's there. It's a fungus so it sort of loiters in your crotch and just waits until you're real sweaty and standing in front of a sell-out crowd of fifty thousand plus a couple million watching on TV and then it starts sending out little "scratch me!" messages to your brain. "C'mon, scratch me!" Earl Weaver was a lot like jock itch.

Even when you think he's not there, he is.

Like in Texas one night. He's suspended. So he's not there. But he's there. Somewhere. It doesn't matter. Nothing can bother me. I'm pitching and I've got no-hitter stuff! I'm throwing hard, throwing strikes, blowing the ball right past these guys.

First inning, they go down on command, one, two, three. Terry Crowley, a really great pinch hitter who studies pitchers to get himself psyched to hit, takes a look at me and says what

I'm thinking. "Jimmy, you can throw a no-hitter tonight." He's right. I feel it. I'm pumped up.

The last thing Earl said to us, pregame and postsuspension, was, "I won't be there [which we all know since we were at the same game as Earl when he lowered the standard for mammal behavior]. Whatever the coaches say, goes! So, don't give them any shit! Otherwise it'll cost you $500!" And this is a man who knows his fines.

Earl isn't allowed in the dugout, so he's up in Hank Peters's box, pacing and hollering and trying to manage from four hundred feet away.

But, like I said, it doesn't matter. I've got no-hitter stuff. Ask Terry Crowley.

Second inning, I'm throwing hard. Really hard. Too hard. I pull a muscle on my left side. Now I am nowhere near rational thinking, which can be good for a pitcher because you just throw, throw, throw. Until you hurt. Which I did.

They get a couple of hits, at first just flukes. A walk, a blooper, a looper down the right field line, off the end of the bat, but they get a couple of runs in the process. By the third inning, I'm struggling. That's how fast no-hit stuff deserts you. No note, no flowers, just poof, gone.

Here comes George Bamberger, who happens to be the nicest guy in the world . . . except for his frequent use of the word *cocksucker* . . . but even that he says as nice as you can say *cocksucker*.

George says, "Earl called down from up there," nodding toward the sky boxes. "He wants me to take you out."

I say, "What for? I can give up a couple more runs. We can still win. Why go to the bullpen?"

George just says, "Earl says you gotta come out."

I say, "*Fuck* Earl! He's sitting up there *phoning* in his ideas. If he was here, I'd tell him the same thing."

George is saying "go" and I'm not moving.

Here comes the umpire, Steve Palermo, who wants to know if we plan to play baseball again soon. I say, "Steve, Earl is suspended."

He says, "Right, we're all thrilled." He looks at the dugout where Earl *isn't* and you can see how he happy is.

And I say, "Earl had a meeting and told us not to give the coaches any shit, and George says Earl called down and said take me out but I don't want to go."

Palermo looks at George and says, "What do you think?"

George, true to form, says, "I don't give a damn. If the cocksucker wants to stay, let the cocksucker stay." (He says it really nicely.)

I say, "But I don't want to get you in trouble with Earl for not following orders."

Palermo decides to play King Solomon. "I'll make the decision for both of you." He asks George, "You want a right-hander or a left-hander?" George goes with the right-hander. And Palermo, yeah, *the umpire,* raises his right hand to signal the bullpen.

Bamberger mumbles something about the how the "relief cocksucker" better get the "batting cocksucker" out and we walk off the mound.

Of course, I didn't want to leave, even if Palermo did bail out Bamberger, 'cause I know it was Earl's call. In fact, this may be the only time in the history of Earl's career that an umpire ever did anything the same way Earl would do it. So, all the way to the dugout, I'm looking up at the boxes, trying to find the little dictator with a phone glued to his ear. I'm just about to the dugout steps and I glare up there and give him one of those tips of the hat. If you can tip your hat sarcastically, I give him an ice-cold, cynical, biting, screw-you tip of the hat. I don't know if he sees it or what, but I can hope.

And hope pays off. I'm icing my arm in the locker room and the phone rings. Clay Reed, the clubhouse man, says I got a call. I know it's Earl but I ask who it is. He says, "It's Earl," and I say, "Earl who?" which Clay doesn't relay to Earl. I know Earl isn't allowed to come into the locker room and yell in person, only by phone, at least until the game is officially over. And I only have to stay nine innings and then I'm out of there. So when he comes thundering in there, which he will because he can't change the way he is, even in a game where he's not really there, I'll be gone. The only thing left will be my uniform and my hat. The hat which I gave him the sarcastic tip of.

Which will annoy him no end. Even when I'm not there. Sort of like jock itch. So we're even.

Coach

Earl had a thing about what he was called. Or rather, what he wasn't called. You could call him manager or skipper or "hey you." But don't call him what Rich Dauer called him.

Dauer had come out of the University of Southern California and then Double A in the mid '70s. He had been hitting around .300 but when he got to the big leagues, he went something like one for forty-one.

At about nonhit number thirty of his no-end-in-sight slump, Dauer flies out or grounds out or fouls out or something that ends with "out," and looks over at Earl in the dugout and says, "Sorry, coach." Earl nods, grimaces, squints, and bites three-quarters of the way through his lower lip.

Then Earl says to me, "Palmer, you want to help the team?"

I say, "Of course, Earl, you know me. I always want to help the team."

"Well, do one thing for me. I don't care if he calls me Earl. I don't care if he calls me Weaver. I don't care if he calls me asshole. Just get him to stop calling me coach!"

See, Dauer had this coach, Coach Dedeaux at Southern

Cal, who was more like a crown prince. He had guys under him who did the coaching but he sort of presided over the realm as the supreme coach and he loved that title . . . "coach."

Earl, on the other hand, had already been a coach and didn't want to be one anymore. He had Bamberger and Frey and Hunter. They were his coaches. He was the manager. And it just gnawed away at his guts, grated him, annoyed him, like cat claws up and down a chalkboard, to be called "coach."

That's why he practically begged me to get Dauer to stop calling him that. And God knows, the last thing I would take any secret, perverse, twisted joy in, would be knowing that something was torturing Earl. Especially if I could do some little thing that would take Earl out of his misery.

Now that I think of it, I might have forgotten to ever ask Dauer to stop calling him coach. Must have slipped my mind.

Pitching, It Rhymes with Bitching

I learned a lot about pitching while Earl Weaver was managing the Orioles. The key word here is *while* he was managing. The missing word is *from,* as in learning from him. I didn't. I learned a lot about a lot of things from Earl Weaver but not about pitching.

I learned from guys like Stu Miller. I sat out in the bullpen with him when I was nineteen and watched and listened. It was like graduate school. And Harvey Haddix, who once pitched an eleven-inning perfect game—and lost, but still, eleven perfect innings! And Robin Roberts, my roommate my first year in the majors, who won over 280 games and went to the Hall of Fame. And huge, six-foot-six Dick Hall, who started as a third baseman and became one of the great control pitchers ever. Charlie Lau, a catcher who caught a lot of great pitchers and who also went on to become a great hitting instructor.

And then there were the guys I pitched alongside of like

Mike Cuellar and Dave McNally. They had off-speed balls and could location-pitch like they had sonar. The real students of the game say, if you have a deceiving windup, location ability, and know when to go off-speed, you can make pitching look easy. Those guys did.

And there were Elrod Hendricks, Rick Dempsey, and Andy Etchebarren, who caught all of us and taught us without even realizing they were conducting class.

Let's see, I must have mentioned seven or eight guys who taught me and I haven't mentioned Earl yet. Oh, don't let me forget the brilliant George Bamberger, our pitching coach. And the almost as brilliant Ray Miller, who was pitching coach after George.

And even guys I taught, I learned from them, too. Like Mike Flanagan and Scotty McGregor and Storm Davis. And opposing pitchers. Like Nolan Ryan. Catfish Hunter.

Gee, that's probably twelve, maybe fourteen guys who I really learned pitching from. Key word, *from*. All *while* Earl was managing.

Dave McNally said it all in deathless words. "The only thing Earl Weaver knows about pitching is that he can't hit it." Which is not to say that Earl didn't *try* to teach me and every other pitcher all about pitching. No, something as important as pitching he wasn't about to leave to the experts.

Elrod Hendricks is an expert. He knows pitching. Especially mine. "Palmer's fastball, he had a fastball that stayed in the zone. Then he had another one that rose, even though they'll try to tell you, in physics, that it's not logical, not even possible, that a fastball would rise. I told those guys, well, you oughta come and catch Palmer one day, and tell me that it doesn't rise, or tell the hitters. I've seen hitters start swinging at the ball in the strike zone, belt high, and the ball would wind up chest high." He was like a professor of pitch-ology. Still is.

In fact, if you took everything Elrod Hendricks knows about pitching and put it together with what Earl knows, you'd have everything Elrod knows by himself.

Elrod was a firsthand observer of the Palmer-Weaver pitching battles. He says Earl knew too little and I knew too much about pitching. Earl wanted every pitch to be a slider, and I wanted hardly any of them to be sliders.

Elrod said I was a pitcher and not just a thrower. A thrower is a guy with a fastball who throws it with everything he's got every time to overpower the batter. A pitcher pitches different to different batters on different days in different cities with different weather and no two differences are alike. And then I moved the fielders around to be where I thought the ball would go.

Earl's strategy was, strike a lot of guys out. No shit.

And Earl wanted to know what every pitch I threw was, and, of course, Elrod knew and mostly wouldn't tell him. And for good reason. When Earl did know what a pitch was, he wanted the pitcher, whoever he was, to throw something else. And he wasn't subtle about it.

Elrod tells about playing in St. Petersburg, Florida. "Tom Phoebus was pitching and he was throwing what Earl must have thought were curveballs. Maybe they were. And he was getting hit. So here comes Lou Brock to bat and Earl yells out to me, 'Tell him'—meaning Phoebus—'to stick that fucking curveball up his ass!' Well, I don't have to tell him because he hears Earl and so does the whole ballpark, including Lou Brock. Lou goes up to bat with a big smile on his face. He knows the next pitch should have been a curve but now he's looking for a high fastball. 'Cause Earl told him. That's what he got. High fastball. And it was gone."

Earl would have just said, "It shouldn't have been a fucking fastball. It should have been a slider." Because he had this kinky attraction to sliders. Maybe it's the word. Sounds kind of dirty. *Slider.* Like something someone does to you for money. Yeah, it was something Earl wanted you to do to every batter.

Mike Flanagan got so sick of Earl's slider fetish, he started lying to him. "Earl's eyesight was so poor that he couldn't really tell the pitches from the dugout. So, if I wasn't pitching, he'd squint at our pitcher and say to me, in that gravely-scratchy-cigarette voice, 'What'd he throw?' At first, I'd tell him what it was. Curve, low. Off-speed. And if the batter got a hit, Earl would curse and snort and say, 'Shoulda been a fuckin' slider!' So, finally, I caught on. And some guy would hit a leadoff home run off our pitcher and Earl would growl, 'What'd he throw?' and I'd say, 'Slider.' Two innings later, an off-the-wall double, and Earl says, 'What'd he throw?' and I say, 'Slider.' And Earl would mutter, 'Ah, the guy got lucky.' Every hit after that, I told him was off a slider."

Flanagan had also nicknamed himself and me. Cy Young, for him, right after he won it, and Cy Old, for me, for obvious reasons, and then he added Cy Clone, for Storm Davis, who was supposed to be like a clone of me. I worked a lot with Storm Davis the way the guys had worked with me. He had the stuff.

You could just tell Storm what to do and he'd do it. At least, I could. We connected. He could pitch real well to left-handers, inside. Tell him to pitch like this to so-and-so. Like that to the next guy. He'd do it. Like you were pushing buttons.

Of course, Earl was in there helping him, too. Encouraging him with discouragement, an Earl specialty (see: "Positive Negative Management," p. 116). One of Earl's favorites was clomping out to the mound and saying to a pitcher in trouble, "Well, fuck!"—as if "fuck" was the guy's name—"If you can't throw strikes here, maybe you can throw 'em in Triple A, back in fucking Rochester!" And then he'd leave the guy alone on the mound with nothing but his glove, his catcher, and a life-size picture of exile to Rochester starting after today's game. No, that guy wasn't tense much.

So, after Earl got done with his "you can't, you don't, you won't, and you never!" approach on Storm, I'd try "you can, you do, you will, and it depends" with him. Storm and I would sit around after games and just talk pitching. The science and the psychology. The American League and the National League styles. Who threw what and why. How hitters react.

Storm was good. And he was part of the Orioles' on-going run of good pitchers and some great ones. He had Boddicker and McGregor with him. And Flanagan.

And they all had Earl. Helping and helping and helping.

One day after one of the other Oriole starters took a beating, Flanagan says he's in the shower just laughing to himself about how mentally wacko Earl had acted toward this pitcher. Flanagan's just laughing, all alone. Earl sees him and hollers, "What's so fucking funny?"

Flanagan says, "Hey, sometimes when we play bad, you just have to laugh."

And Earl says, "Oh yeah? You ain't got nothing to throw at them. You got nothing to get them out!" That ought to boost Mike since he's due to pitch the next game.

But Earl isn't done. He spins around and sees another O's pitcher and stabs his finger at that guy. "You see this guy, here? He's got shit!" Well, that takes care of another starter. "And you, you're all supposed to be good pitchers but you've got junk!"

That about covers the whole rotation. All fueled up with confidence.

So, how come the Orioles had such good pitching if Earl knew almost nothing about pitching and what he did know was mostly wrong? Earl couldn't coach pitchers, but he could find them. He could spot them, trade for them, stick with them. He might have driven them crazy, but he knew which ones to drive crazy.

Earl stuck by his pitchers . . . and his fielders and his hitters. When you went to spring training, if you made his team, and it was tough to break in, but if you did, in Elrod's words, and he's a coach now and has to do the same, "On Weaver's teams, there were no small men. Everybody was important. He'd say, 'I'm taking the best twenty-five guys, and every one of you is going to be an integral part of this club. Each one of you is going to help us win the pennant.'"

Hell, Earl could actually care about a player, even a pitcher, as long as he thought nobody was watching. Flanagan caught him once. "There was a cut-rate place in Milwaukee where you get suits and ties. And we had called up Eric Bell, a young pitcher right from Double A. We had a sport coat rule and the kid didn't have a sport coat or much of anything for that matter. Earl took him to this cut-rate place and I happened to be there. There was Earl, buying the kid a suit. Anybody else would've said, 'Hi, Mike.' Earl grabbed me outside and said, 'You tell anybody, I'll release you.'"

He was there for his players all the way. He just couldn't show it. It's why he hung in with pitchers for CGPs, which don't count much anymore but used to. Complete games pitched, win or lose. And even though he didn't know what pitch you should throw, he did know when to keep a pitcher in and when to pull a pitcher. When to point to the bullpen, like he did with me, and say, "You see anybody out there better than you to finish this game?"

"No."

"Then finish the fucking game."

He was there for me when I was having trouble in '82. Earl didn't tell me in so many words that he was there, and he never would. I got it second-hand, but a reliable second-hand, that Earl told Hank Peters, "This guy has done more for this organization and this ball club than you'll ever do."

And there was more. "I cannot put this guy on the bench.

I'd rather you just release him. I'm not going to sit him down here and embarrass him that way.

"This guy has kept my pocket filled with money. He kept me in a job. I will not do it! I refuse to do it!"

If I had asked Earl, to his face, if he stood up for me, he would have said, "Just pitch. I got twenty-four other guys to worry about." One of his favorite lines.

So, he pitched me. He put me in the bullpen and brought me in as much as he could. Then he started me. And when I started winning, and we got in a race to the wire, he reminded Hank Peters as loud and as often as he could.

That's why the last game I pitched under Earl, for the division, against Milwaukee was such a rough loss for both of us. We weren't just trying to win. We were proving something to a certain front office guy.

And that was Earl's last season, his retirement year. He could have backed off. If he had been somebody else. But Earl stuck by his guns . . . and his guys. Like in '72 he'd write Don Buford out of the lineup at breakfast and then on the drive to the stadium remember all the times Buford saved our butts and have him right back in there. Same with Terry Crowley. That's how Terry always seemed to be the twenty-fifth guy to make the team.

And if an umpire tossed one of our guys out of a game, Earl, in the middle of all that ranting and raving, would rant some guilt-heavy logic for that ump. "I put that player in to help win a ball game, and you've taken that away from me. You've taken that away from the fans. You've deprived this guy of earning a living for his family."

See, Earl Weaver was a manager.

But he still didn't know shit about pitching. And worse, he didn't know that he didn't know. Not that it was a secret. He may rank as the only guy who was supposed to be on our side but who drove the pitchers so crazy by second-guessing the umpire so much that the umpire would look at Earl every time he made a call, just waiting for a fight. He made his own pitchers and catchers so crazy that at least one Oriole pitcher and one Oriole catcher I know of said to umpires, "Come on, throw his ass out! He's driving us all nuts. Please throw him out. You'll call 'em better and we'll have a nice quiet game."

That's right. His players asked, begged, the ump to eject their own manager. Not for managing, for what he didn't know about pitching.

But I refuse to name names of who would do such a thing . . . Elrod and Mike.

1978

Uh-Oh, Maturity

One of us was starting to grow up. The other one was still acting like a baby. I say the baby was him. He says it was me. But it was him. He was too much of a baby to admit that I was more grown-up than he was.

Nineteen seventy-eight was Jim Palmer and Earl Weaver's tenth season together.

On May 5, Weaver started Palmer against the Indians and, at the age of thirty-two, Palmer gained his two hundredth win.

Only two other Orioles had hit the two hundred mark, Milt Pappas and Robin Roberts, and neither of them did it exclusively with the Birds as Palmer had. And, of course, all but a handful of Palmer's wins were under the management of Earl Weaver.

Palmer once again was selected for the All-Star team and once again was the American League starter.

Earl Weaver pitched Palmer against Detroit on September 23, and Jim gained his twentieth victory of the season.

During the '78 season, Palmer also entered the ranks of another illustrious group, "three thousand inning" pitchers. And he won his third Gold Glove.

I Guess I Was Trying, after All

You can get a short version of my entire career, a sort of *Cliff's Notes to the Palmer Saga,* all in the month of May, 1978. It was like, *Palmer, the Miniseries.* May of '78 had it all.

Starting at the end of the month (just because it would be too simple and not like me to start at the beginning) on May 28, in Cleveland, I pitched a 3–0 shutout. It was my two-hundredth career win. A pretty big moment. At the age of thirty-two, I joined a semielite club of active pitchers like Jim Kaat, Gaylord Perry, Catfish Hunter, and Tom Seaver. I got a four-tiered cake with two hundred candles and champagne and reporters and lots of kind words. "Phenomenal, he's phenomenal!"

Quick quiz. Who said that?

I'll give you a clue. It's the same guy who stormed out to the mound a mere three weeks earlier, while I was personally hosting a Walks-R-Us extravaganza for the benefit of the Minnesota Twins, and hollered, "Jesus H. Christ, are you fucking trying?!"

One more clue: It's also the very same guy who went apeshit when I left not only the mound, at his request, but the stadium, at mine, before the end of the game, breaking a club rule. My only excuses were that I was pissed off at (1) Dempsey's error, Belanger's error, Billy Smith's error, and other nonhelp from my team, (2) my own arm-full-of-cortisone, anywhere-but-the-strike-zone, horseshit pitching, (3) and mostly, being asked, in all seriousness, if I was *"fucking trying." Was I fucking trying?! Was I fucking trying?!* I still get crazy when I think of that question.

But back to the quiz. The kind and caring comments couldn't have come from the same human being (to use the term loosely) who made the crude and coarse comments. Could they? Who could say them? Well, that same quotable fella said, a mere twenty-three days, three shutouts, and 27²/₃ no-run innings later, on the occasion of win number two hundred, "We needed every damn one of those scoreless innings . . . because we haven't been scoring ourselves." Suddenly back to being sweet, even bordering on sensitive.

Time's up. Your answer, please. Hint: The initials are EW, and Edward Bennett Williams hadn't bought the team yet.

Bzzzz! Earl Weaver. Correct!

The ups and the downs of our whole relationship all in May of '78. My arm was hurt (as usual) and I was disgusted at being underpaid (as usual) and there were trade talks (as usual) and the team was playing lousy (*not* as usual) and Earl and I both wanted to win so bad we were at each other and with each other constantly.

I went, as the *Baltimore Sun* said, "Over the Hill" on May 7 after the Minnesota game, and left the clubhouse, sending the USS *Earl* into orbit.

I then pitched three shutouts, had all those scoreless innings, won number two hundred, and Earl was gushing.

When we were celebrating the two-hundredth in the clubhouse (no, I didn't leave early that day), he was the first to shake my hand. He said, "Remember, a hundred of those are mine."

I wasn't surprised and said so. "I figured Earl would take credit for 181." That'd be all of them except the ones when I wasn't playing for him.

The reporters asked about our relationship (as usual), and I said, "He only yells at me because he knows I'll forgive him."

Earl said, "We spent ten years together. That's longer than some marriages. Hell, I've had two that haven't lasted as long as that, myself."

That was May of '78. Yeah, I was fucking trying. I was trying when I walked four guys in a row against the Twins. I was trying when I shutout the Indians for number two hundred. And of course, I was trying Earl and he was trying me.

Sliders

I have a simple philosophy about pitching, which is that you don't go to the batter's weakness until you have to. Try to get him with your good pitches before you go to his bad pitches, that is, his weaknesses.

We're playing Texas in the middle of May of 1978 and the guy who had been our third-base coach, Billy Hunter, was managing the Rangers. I've got a 2–0 lead going into the bottom of the eighth. And John Lowenstein, who was playing with the Rangers at the time, hits a double off the top of the center field fence.

There are two outs, runners at second and third, and Juan Beniquez is up. So far, he's flied out to deep right and singled to right, and they were on fastballs, away. I figure, I better put my philosophy to work, the second part of it anyway, which is, since my good pitches are not working, it's time to go to his weakness—which is fastballs up and in.

Beniquez is a pretty good breaking-ball hitter and a better fastball hitter, at least he is based on the evidence of the last two times I saw the ball fly off his bat past my head. So, I get two strikes on him and I throw to him, up and in. The pitch breaks his bat and he hits this little looper into left center where Pat Kelly, our left fielder, is playing him to pull, which is somewhere between kind of out of position and a lot out of position, and the ball drops in.

The score is tied 2–2 and they have the potential winning run, Beniquez, at second. But, and this is another part of my philosophy, I figure it's not over until they score more runs than you. Having runs in scoring *position* doesn't count. So I get the next guy out. And my philosophy is intact. Wounded, but intact.

I come walking into the dugout, which is an old-time chasmy thing with a watercooler dividing it so about a third of it is where the manager and coaches and maybe a really dumb player would sit. The rest of it, toward the pit and heading for the clubhouse, is where the rest of the players sit. I put my glove on the team side of the watercooler and there's Earl, really pissed-off, sitting on the pissed-off side of the watercooler. As I reach for my jacket, Earl growls, "The rest of the fucking league is throwing sliders to .166 hitters!"

A .166 hitter? Beniquez's stats had come up on the scoreboard and it said .166. But he's not really .166. He hit .269, .257, and .291 the last three years, and he's on his way to .300. It's early in the season; he's a platoon hitter; and he hasn't had that many at bats. He's not .166. He's .300 in a .166 disguise. It's like saying the Boston Strangler has a nice handshake.

But I don't know if Earl is really talking to me or to himself or to nobody. Because when we're playing, Earl is so deep into winning that he enters the Earl Universe. Maybe the sound of my glove hitting the bench triggered Earl's inner voices, or maybe Earl is about to answer himself. I don't say anything. Earl hollers, "I said, the rest of the fucking league is throwing sliders to .166 hitters."

I guess he was talking to me.

And he's talking about sliders. Which is not surprising since they're his favorite pitch. Not mine.

A few words about me, Earl, and sliders. In 1968, when I had hurt my arm, Earl watched me pitch in the Instructional League and I was giving up ten runs and fourteen hits a game. I had gotten past the torn rotator cuff, but I had a lot of inflammation and, until I took the anti-inflammatory pills, I couldn't throw hard. In plain language, I was pitching shitty. And in Earl's language, "worse than shitty."

He says, "I wouldn't give a nickel for Palmer's chance of getting back to the big leagues. He's gotta come up with a slider."

Now Earl really did think the slider was the greatest pitch ever. He loved sliders. Deeply. He had an unnatural attraction to sliders. Probably, when he came through the minors, he couldn't hit sliders. He couldn't hit much of anything, so for sure he couldn't hit sliders.

But to me, it was a dangerous pitch. If you throw it right, it's great, but if you make a bad pitch with it, if you hang it, it gives the batter a huge edge. It increases his bat speed, and if he connects, the ball goes a long, long way, and a long, long way in baseball is the same direction as the seats, and that's bad. I don't throw sliders much. Only a fraction more than never.

So when he repeats ". . . throw sliders to .166 hitters . . ." I say, "Excuse me?" which to Earl is like saying "Fuck off, asshole!"

And he says, "You heard me," which, to me, must have been like "Fuck off, asshole!" So basically, we have all the makings of a highly intellectual conversation.

I say, "Earl, I'm trying to do my best and that's all I can do."

And he says, "It's not fucking good enough."

I look at him and say, "Earl, you have two options," and I look down the left field line toward the bullpen. "First, if you have somebody better, bring him in. And second, if you think it's so easy, here's my glove. You go out and pitch."

It's safe to say, that comment annoyed him. He leaps up (at least, I think he did because now his face was higher) and he screams, into my chest, "So you're quitting?"

"No, Earl, I'm not quitting."

"Well, get the fuck out of here," he says, and he walks me down to the other end of the bench while everybody, I mean our team and the whole Texas Ranger's team, is watching every minute of this like it's the "Who Shot J.R.?" episode of *Dallas*. This is way more interesting than baseball.

He sort of moves me down by the steps, toward the tunnel

where all the equipment is, and he's yelling and screaming and his neck is pulsing . . . he's pretty much acting like usual.

And I say, "Earl, can't we discuss this in a mature way?"

Bad suggestion.

He goes more berserk. Or berserker. Or, in Earl-ese, fucking berserk. "If you're so fucking mature, get out there and pitch."

And I say, "Okay."

We hadn't scored, so the score is still tied at 2–2. The first Ranger up hits a ground ball to Mark Belanger. Mark catches it but loses his footing and it's not an error, it's a base hit.

Now it's a bunt situation, and you just want to throw the ball down the middle, let the guy bunt, give you an out, even though it moves the runner into scoring position. Then you can decide who you want to pitch to, either the next guy, or walk him to set up a double play and pitch to the guy after him. But with all these options and plans, I'm trying so hard to throw the ball down the middle that I throw it everywhere but. I walk the guy.

So now, it's men on first and second and, instead of one out, it's nobody out. Another bunt situation. And I walk the next guy, too.

I think I'm under control, but you'd have to say my pitching indicates otherwise. Maybe it was the argument with Earl. Sometimes a screaming match with a lunatic can make you lose your focus . . . a little.

The bases are loaded and I get a visitor on the mound. Old Yeller, Earl. He hollers up from two feet below me. I refuse to step down off the rubber and give him the satisfaction of only being one foot shorter than me. I look down; he looks up. Heavy glaring.

He brings in Don Stanhouse. I get a ticket to the locker room.

Stanhouse is our top reliever. I'm listening on the radio.

He's about to face Al Oliver (who was on the 1971 Pirates team that beat us in the World Series and who is going to finish his career with 2,700 hits). Oliver hits a sacrifice fly. A run scores. They get a couple more hits and more runs and the bases are loaded.

Guess who's back at the plate? Juan Beniquez. It's now 5–2 and Stanhouse is still pitching. I hear the radio announcer say, "The wind up, the pitch. It's . . . a slider and Beniquez hits it high to left field . . . back . . . way back . . ." The ball hits the top of the left field wall and misses being a grand slam by an inch or two, tops. And the radio announcer adds for good measure, "Looks like Stanhouse hung a slider."

Now, I do not like to lose games. I do not like to give up earned runs. And at this point, in this losing game, I'm getting credit for giving up five runs. So I'm not happy about much.

But I'm happy about one thing. The slider that Earl wanted me to throw, the slider he got Stanhouse to throw, the one that ended up being a triple, which was a near–grand slam, the slider that brought in three more runs. I'm pretty happy about that little detail. The slider detail. Or did I mention that already?

So I'm in the locker room and Earl comes flying in like the Tazmanian Devil from Looney Tunes with an actual cloud of dust behind him, and says, "Palmer! We gotta talk in my office!"

I go to his office and he says, "Palmer! We gotta talk."

And I say, "You said that, Earl."

And he says, "That's 'cause we gotta talk."

And I say, "I don't want to talk about it."

And he says, "We gotta fucking talk." So I figure he really means it.

So I talk. "Earl, I've been here twelve years. We've been together a long time. You've done a good job managing, but

I can't handle coming back to the bench and you're second-guessing everybody and you're negative and you're yelling and everybody's wrong but you."

"You're wrong, Palmer!" he bellows, ignoring all irony. "Why don't you just quit?"

"I don't want to quit," I say. "I need the money. I need paychecks. I have kids and a divorce."

"So we can't talk about this?" Earl yells.

"No, there's nothing to talk about. I'll talk to Hank Peters [the GM] when we get back. It's best that I get traded."

"You mean, you don't want to talk about it?" The man is either legally deaf or monumentally stubborn . . . or both.

"Earl, we've been talking . . . we've been yelling . . . for ten years. It's probably best for both of us. You can get somebody else for me."

"So we can't talk about this?" Earl stares. "Then get the fuck outa here." He gets up and glares over me in my chair. Then he grabs the door and throws it open so hard, it closes again. He does it again, just as hard. And it closes. So I open it to leave. And he gives me one of those low bow kind of gestures, very grandiose, as I walk out.

I head for my locker, past the showers and the sinks and the training room on the other side. Behind me I hear this thunder of cleats across the tile like a herd of tap dancers. But it's just one dancer, a really pissed-off dancer, Earl Weaver.

"We're having a team meeting!" he hollers to everybody. "Everybody sit the fuck down."

Guys are eating and dressing and talking. But they sit the fuck down. We haven't been playing very well. We lost seven of eight on this lousy road trip and we're supposed to be contenders, chasing the Yankees who had won the Series in 1977.

Earl paces. He stares. He looks over everybody, real slow. Then he says, "Okay, who wants to be traded?"

Nobody says a word. Nobody moves. And nobody knows what the fuck he's talking about it.

"C'mon, raise your hand if you want to be traded." Not a twitch from anybody. He keeps rolling. "Because this guy"— and he shoots his finger at me like a spear—"this guy wants to be traded!"

Just like that, he's alienated me from twenty-four other guys. I'm the guy who wants out. I'm the one who doesn't want to be part of the team.

Then Earl goes on to give a speech about how the team has to be more intense, how we have to have better pitching defense, peppered with "cocksuckers," "dumb fucks," and "assholes." All in all, he gives one of his better speeches.

I don't say a word. And Earl heads for his office, where he attacks the leg of a defenseless postgame fried chicken.

I walk down the hall with a towel around me and see Earl gnawing and clawing and snarling at this dead chicken and, maybe it was seeing the bird carcass, I say, "Earl, that was chickenshit, really chickenshit."

I mean, I didn't tell him I wanted to leave because I didn't like the other guys or the team. I said I had had enough of all of his bullshit. I keep walking.

All of a sudden I've got the thundering tap dancer behind me again, only this time he's got the chicken leg in his teeth and there's a vein in his neck that looks like I-95 from Baltimore to Miami and Jimmy Frey, our bench coach, and Ray Miller, the pitching coach, are right behind him because they think there's going to be a fight. I look at Earl and I say again, "It was really chickenshit, Earl."

The trainer, Ralph Salvon, is as still as a statue. Everybody is. Like they're frozen, waiting. Long silence. Everybody stares at everybody. Earl turns around and goes to his office.

Afterward, the sportswriters get wind of something and

they're asking what's going on. What do I tell them? I say Earl just didn't care for some of my pitching selections, which is the truth, in a total bullshit kind of way. I also told them I had never seen Earl so tall.

The next night I go to the ballpark and, if you're going to sit on the bench, you can't sit all that far from Earl, so I sit and don't say anything. The next day I go down to the bullpen, do my running and throwing, and sit as close to Elrod Hendricks as I can and don't say anything again.

And after the game, Earl calls me into his office. He takes a pause that lasts about an inning or two and he says, "Jim, I want to thank you for handling it like you did."

Earl was sorry. For him, anyway. And, if you know him, it's okay. But you don't throw sliders just because he couldn't hit them.

A Short Lesson in How to Not Throw a Grand Slam

It's 1978 and I'm about 3,000 major league innings into having never given up a grand slam. I had no intention of starting at 3,001. Or ever. (I was going to go on to pitch 3,945 innings and they could get their walks and doubles and even three-run homers but no major league grand slams. Zero.) Maybe it was the indelible memory of the one grand slam I did throw, in the minors. . . .

In Rochester, I had listened to Earl when he said to throw the ball "right down the middle" to a guy named Johnny Bench even though I didn't agree with Earl and was pretty sure that "right down the middle" was a bad pitch to throw to this guy, Johnny Bench. But I did what my manager said. And in fairness to Earl, it only scored the usual four runs that come at no extra charge with a grand slam.

So when the chance came up again to experience the thrill

of the ball escaping from the park at high speed and a four-man parade marching across home plate, well, I had a kind of avoidance reaction. I said to myself, no way!

However, I wasn't throwing anything particularly good on this particular day in 1978. We weren't hitting either. It'll come as no surprise that Earl was in a hemorrhoid-shitty mood.

I'm having trouble with my change-up and George Bamberger, the pitching coach, says if you're not throwing a good change-up you should try to open up your front shoulder to get the ball to move more from left to right . . . so you get more action on the ball. Okay, I try it, and whatever action I got on the ball was nothing compared to the action that John Lowenstein got. He got home-run-off-the-foul-pole action.

Now it's later on and we're behind 3–0 and they've got a runner on first. They try a bunt, and Doug DeCinces throws the ball over to first, actually just plain *over* first; the runners go to second and third so first is open. There's one out. Lowenstein is up again.

And I get a social call from Earl at the mound. Earl says, "Walk Lowenstein." A bell goes off in my head. No, an alarm. No, those World War II air raid sirens go off. Bad idea—bad idea—bad idea!

Part of being a good pitcher is you always know who's on deck and what the lineup is and what each one of them has done against you, recently and sometimes back to Little League. You're prepared. You try to have a game plan so you know who you can get out and how and when—stuff like that which may keep you from losing or at least from getting totally obliterated and thereby putting you in retirement a decade or two earlier than you planned.

The point is, as I said, I had never thrown a grand slam in my major league career, I had no intention of throwing a grand slam in that career, and this advice Earl is giving me leads toward the very thing that is neither good for the score nor my career . . . the previously mentioned grand slam. Plus the fact that we hadn't scored four runs—the exact number of runs required to make up for the other team's four grand slam runs—in the last month.

I'm way ahead of Earl. But I'm not getting through. He's already figured it all out and come to a happy ending, which, by the way, is a fantasy. A good fantasy but still a fantasy, as in Snow White, Cinderella, the Frog Prince, etc. Earl says, "You walk Lowenstein to get to Al Oliver and you can get out of the inning with one pitch."

Sometimes that works. Sometimes you do that. You walk the bases loaded, like if you have a sinker ball pitcher whose pitches, if they get hit, turn into ground balls. He can load the bases and get somebody to hit a grounder and boom, you got a double play and you're out of the inning, just like Earl said in his fantasy, in one pitch. Happy ending.

I don't want to rain all over Earl's fantasy but . . . there's one problem. I'm a high fastball pitcher. When they hit me, they don't hit a lot of ground balls. And if they do, it's a line drive on one hop, which means it's hit well, which means it's hard to field, which means the double play is, shall we say, a fantasy. I actually could give Earl ten or twelve, no, make that forty-six reasons why this idea of walking Lowenstein to get to Al Oliver and hoping he hits a grounder into a double play is not a wise move.

Around reason number thirty-eight, Earl interrupts and says, "Jimmy, maybe you *will* throw a double play grounder."

I come back, "When's the last time I did that?"

Earl is silent, a rare and wonderful moment.

I say, "Earl, you want me to walk Lowenstein to get to Oliver [who has about 2,700 hits by this time in his career and is probably just itching for that grand slam] with the bases loaded?"

Earl says, "Yeah."

I hand Earl the ball and say, "You want to walk Lowenstein to get to Al Oliver, you do it."

He looks at me from down where he is and says, "Just walk the fucking guy," hands the ball back to me, and runs off the mound. So I guess I have to do it.

Now this whole time there's one other guy listening, Rick Dempsey, our catcher. But Dempsey is so intense, so into the game, that he doesn't hear all this back-and-forth bullshit and he sure as hell doesn't retain it. He just wants to crouch behind the plate, hold up some fingers, and play like a madman. Anyway, I walk Lowenstein. The bases are loaded. Just like I didn't want them to be. And Oliver is up, just like I didn't want him to be.

Dempsey comes out to the mound and I say, "Demper, let's get this straight. I've never thrown a grand slam. I don't intend to throw a grand slam."

Dempsey nods.

Jim Sundberg, a right-hander who didn't have much power, was on deck. I go on, "Look, we're gonna lose, but we gotta get out of this."

And Dempsey nods again and looks right through me because he's so intense, he doesn't remember any of this long-winded conversation with Earl. He just wants to crouch and hold up fingers and play baseball.

I say, "Even if I have to walk Oliver and walk a run in, I don't care. I'm not throwing him anything on the inside part of the plate that he can turn into a home run. I'll get to Sundberg and get out of the inning."

Dempsey nods and looks through me again.

I keep going, "Just sit on the *outside* corner and we'll throw him four pitches a little bit off the plate. If he wants to swing at a shit sandwich, let him have a picnic."

Dempsey goes back to the plate. I look for the sign. I'm

pitching from the stretch position with the ball in my glove on my left side.

Okay, Dempsey gives me the fastball sign. But he doesn't give me any indication of where he wants it, like outside, where I told him fifteen seconds ago, I was going to put it . . . and the next three pitches. I figure, well, we just talked about it so he'll move to the outside of the plate anyway. I look at the runner at third to make sure he doesn't have too big a lead and I start my hands, bringing my glove up, about to start my windup . . . and Dempsey, instead of moving off the plate, to the left since Oliver is a left-handed hitter, moves up and in. He's crouched; he's holding up some fingers; and he's playing intense baseball. But he's not doing what we said!

So, I make this subtle move to start my windup and I step off the rubber, straight back toward second base, the totally legal way to do it, if you haven't actually started your windup, and I hear from behind me in short center, "Balk!" It's Joe Brinkman, the crew chief who's umpiring second base, with his hands up, calling a balk.

A balk! That means the runners advance. The runner at first goes to second, the runner at second to third, and the guy at third scores. The bases are no longer loaded! After Earl's fantasy plan of walking Lowenstein to get to Al "2,700 Hits" Oliver with the bases loaded and my plan of throwing four off the corner of the plate, the bases aren't full anymore.

I'm actually smiling. Every TV set that was tuned to Oriole baseball saw a pitcher who got called for a balk, smiling.

It's safe to say Earl wasn't smiling. He had fantasized, or visualized, this whole thing. And, in his mind, it all worked. The walk, the double-play grounder, one pitch and you're out of the inning. He saw it all. And the happy ending that went with it.

As it turned out, Oliver popped up. (I pitched to him

since the bases weren't loaded and since Dempsey kept sitting on the inside of the plate anyway.) Then the next guy flew out and I held them to four runs.

PS. Those four runs came one at a time, not four at once. When they all come at once, they call that a grand slam. I never did throw one of those.

You Can Pitch a No-Hitter If Your Fielders Catch Everything

I was accused of moving fielders around when I was pitching. Actually having the nerve to turn around to, say, the left fielder, and waving him toward the foul line two and a half feet or back toward the wall, or over three steps to his right and in a foot or so, not so far, whoa, right there. Like an orchestra conductor or something. Like I knew where the ball was going to be hit. That would take real gall, guts, balls, to do something like that.

So I only did it when I thought I had to.

When I had guys like Frank Robinson playing behind me, even after he hurt his arm, he already knew where to be. Not just where the guy was likely to hit it, but how I was probably pitching him, not in general like high and inside, but pitch by pitch and where those pitches would go if they got hit.

Same with Paul Blair, only more so. He was practically in my head, on the mound, when I pitched, which is why so many balls seemed to head for his glove.

And Brooks Robinson at third. I never told him where to play. If he thought he should be in the second stall of the bathroom in the locker room, I'd just pitch, and he'd kick open the door and catch the ball.

But later we got guys, good guys, who just didn't always play that way. They might not know, for instance, that if they're playing a step or two to the opposite field and you're behind the batter two balls and no strikes or three and one, and you have a big lead in the game, you're probably going to take a little off the pitch to make sure the batter puts it in play, and the fielders have to know to shift a couple of steps and play for the batter to pull.

It isn't just how to play a batter, it's how to play the batter during the course of the at bat. Maybe three different ways. And it's all a gamble, but it's either a smart bet or a long shot.

So you don't move fielders who know where to move, guys whose feet are wired to their instincts which are telephathically connected to the pitcher's brain and gut which are really an extension of the catcher's mind, memory, and which fingers he holds up.

But the other two hundred or so players who are in the majors, who don't know all that stuff, at least not yet . . . those guys I would sometimes have the nerve to move. And, yeah, it aggravated some of them. And when they got aggravated, it aggravated Earl. And then he got aggravated with me. But that was normal. So, I moved the fielders around sometimes.

I'll give you an example. Not to spoil a surprise ending, but it's going to be one where I was right to do it.

We're playing Oakland in Baltimore and on deck the A's have this guy, Dave Revering, who hit home runs off me a lot. I'd throw a fastball and he'd hit a home run. I couldn't get my breaking ball over with him, so I'd go back to fastballs and he'd go back to home runs.

We have a 2–0 lead, and ahead of Revering is Dell Alston. Jimmy Frey, meanwhile, is our first-base coach and one of the great fielder-mover-arounders of all time. So, he's watching all this from the dugout.

I'm behind Dell Alston two balls and no strikes. He's a left-handed pull hitter. With a 2–0 count, the last thing I want to do is let this guy get a free pass so that Revering will have a shot at a two-run homer instead of his already-annoying habit of one-run homers. Alston may get on with a base hit but no free rides.

Kenny Singleton is playing Alston in straightaway right field. Which is okay right up until my next pitch. The one after the 2–0 count. Because now I'm going to throw him a fastball and he's a good fastball hitter and he may even know I'm going to throw him a fastball. I just want Singleton to know what I'm going to throw and what can happen when I do.

I look out to right field and look at Kenny, who's still playing straightaway on this beautiful Sunday afternoon in Baltimore. I motion him a couple of steps toward a pull hit for a left-hander, in other words, closer to the right field line.

And on this beautiful Sunday afternoon, I turn around and throw a fastball to Dell Alston. And he does seem to know it's coming and he hits a line drive, actually he pulls a line drive toward the right field line.

Kenny Singleton has to make an unbelievable play to catch the ball. He has to lift his glove to his chest. A good ten-inch gesture. He doesn't move his feet. He doesn't bend. He doesn't stretch. He puts his glove in front of his chest . . . mostly to prevent Alston's line drive from imbedding itself there permanently.

Jimmy Frey comes up to me afterward and says, "Boy, you make me look good when you do that."

And then he tells me that when I did it and when Kenny caught the ball, Earl leaned over to Frey and said, "Shit, now he knows he's smarter than we are."

But I would never gloat. I'd just remember the story twenty years later, Earl.

Don't worry. I also remember what the sportswriters said after I gave up nine home runs in back-to-back series against Boston. "The next time Palmer wants to move an outfielder, maybe he should move them up into the bleachers so they could save those home runs he's throwing."

Believe me, I would've if I could've.

I guess I would have aggravated the other guys and Earl a lot less if I never moved them around. If I never nudged a guy left or right or in or out. But then, if the ball had gone to where I was going to move him but hadn't moved him, then I'd have to put up with Earl being aggravated about a hit or a run or, worse, not winning. So I picked the lesser of two aggravations.

1979

Almost

Earl and I argued with each other to the top of our division. We argued to first place and the American League pennant. We argued to the World Series against the Pirates and nearly argued all the way to the championship. Maybe if we had just argued a little bit more . . .

After eight twenty-win seasons, Jim Palmer was Earl Weaver's natural choice for Opening Day against the White Sox. And Jim got the victory, 5–3.

Weaver and Palmer had a good year. Weaver and the Orioles had a great year.

Jim won his fourth Gold Glove.

The Orioles took on California for the American League pennant. Palmer started Game 1, allowed only three runs in nine innings, and was relieved by Don Stanhouse, who got the win. The Birds won the pennant, three games to one.

Weaver led his team into the World Series against a powerful Pittsburgh Pirates team. In Game 2, Weaver started Palmer against Bert Blyleven. Jim pitched seven innings and gave up two runs and was relieved by Tippy Martinez and Don Stanhouse. The Orioles lost the game, 3–2.

But they came back in the Series and went to Game 6. Again, Weaver started Palmer. In a heart-breaking finish to the season, the Pirates beat Baltimore, 4–0, to win the championship.

Positive-Negative Management

Earl managed by the Positive-Negative method. Which is not to be confused with the Negative-Positive method.

The Positive-Negative approach meant Earl would always tell you what not to do, how not screw up, tell you all the things you were already doing wrong, or order you to do fewer things wrong. And he thought that would somehow motivate you to do better.

The Negative-Positive approach would be telling you something good, but telling you in a bad way. Like, "Nice hit! It's about time you got lucky."

But that would be much too positive for Earl.

Nobody knows when the Weaver Positive-Negative style of baseball management first showed itself, but there is evidence dating back at least to 1964 in Aberdeen, South Dakota. Earl is managing the Double A team and they have this kid, Steve Cosgrove, they drafted from the Milwaukee organization. He's a bonus baby and, along with Frankie Bertaina, these two guys are the hotshots of the minors. They have big motel rooms and fancy cars and sharkskin suits and pinky rings. Actual pinky rings!

I'm playing A ball and my roommate is Davey Leonhard. Cal Ripken Sr. is our manager and we're going to face this kid, Cosgrove. We have what I thought, at the time, was a real good team. We've won twenty-five out of our first twenty-nine and the last fourteen in a row.

Meanwhile, I'm coaching first base. Cosgrove strikes out everybody in the first inning. I come into the dugout and say to Davey, "Did you see the stuff this guy has? High fastball, curveball falling off the table, low and away fastball, great control. He's got everything. How are we ever gonna get to the big leagues if they throw like that in Double A?"

And Davey says, "Don't worry about a thing."

I say, "What do you mean, don't worry about a thing? If this is the way they throw in Double A, how are we ever going to get to the big leagues?"

Davey says, "Just don't worry. When he throws the first pitch that isn't a strike, Earl Weaver jumps up on the top step of the dugout like a rabid chipmunk. Then, when he throws ball two, Earl starts yelling at the top of his lungs, 'Here we go again! You're gonna walk the entire ballpark!'"

Well, Cosgrove finally throws a ball, and right on cue, Earl leaps up to the top step. Then comes ball two, and Earl yells out just about word for word what Davey predicted. And Cosgrove falls apart. Ball three, ball four . . . and the parade begins.

See, Earl figured telling the guy he was starting to fuck up and catching him in the early stages of fucking up would motivate the guy to stop fucking up. Like the guy was fucking up on purpose or something.

But to Earl, it was motivation. Now the guy knows what *not* to do. Earl hated walks.

But it never occurred to him that his way might not be the best way to prevent walks. Ask John Flinn.

Flinn was a terrific pitcher with Rochester in Triple A. He had a good curve, good control, nice, sinking fastball. When he was relaxed. Relaxed is important because here's what happens when a pitcher gets tense. You can't get the ball out of your fingertips. You grip the ball too tightly so if you're a sinker ball pitcher, the ball doesn't sink. The pitch ends up being fat and juicy, no movement, no sinking, just sitting there, waist high, like dessert. So instead of the hitters hitting the top of the ball and getting grounders to the third baseman who throws to first for the easy out, you get dead-center-of-the-ball line drives and home runs and bad stuff like that. So, again, "relaxed" is important.

Flinn gets called up and we're playing in Cleveland in the early '80s sometime. We're behind seven or eight runs and it's the sixth inning. Earl is already in a mood where if one more thing goes wrong you should be really glad he doesn't work in the Pentagon or anyplace near that red button.

Flinn gets the call from the bullpen. And he walks the first guy. Earl gives him a long-distance scowl-and-mutter combo from the dugout steps. Tension enters; relaxed is in retreat.

Flinn walks another guy. Earl stomps out to the mound to tell Flinn, in person, about a half inch from his face, how much he hates walks. On the off chance that Flinn likes them. If he wasn't really tense before, he is now. He's wired like a violin. Relaxed is no longer in the same hemisphere as John Flinn.

Flinn bears down. And the next guy hits a double. Good-bye Flinn. He's coming off the mound, battered, beaten, and searching for safe harbor. He looks for a place to sit, as far away from wherever Weaver sits as possible. He picks a spot between me and Mike Flanagan.

Weaver trudges into the dugout and, instead of heading for his spot at the other end, makes his way toward us. He looks right between me and Flanagan, which means right at Flinn, and says, "I thought he was supposed to be on our side!" Flinn's head falls into his hands.

Earl harrumphs down to his end of the bench, convinced he's given Flinn a goal to aim for next time. *Not* being horrible. The Negative that's supposed to be Positive.

Like the time when I can't seem to throw anything but high pitches. One high, two high, three high, walk. High, high, high. Walk, walk, walk. Everything is high, and Earl says, "At least *bounce* one on the plate so I know you're trying." In the Negative-Positive logic, throw a ball low, instead of all balls high. Do something bad that's different than the bad stuff I'm already doing so he'll know I'm trying not to do bad stuff. Huh?

Positive-Negative. That's what he used on Bobby Grich. Bobby hit thirty-nine home runs in Rochester, but he had trouble getting started in the majors. Everytime he'd hit a long fly ball that got caught, Earl would wait for Grich to come back to the dugout and say, "Home run in Rochester." Very subtle. He might as well have said, "Either do it here or go back." Which he said to plenty of pitchers.

Then when Rich Dauer got into this streak where he went one for his first forty-one at bats, Earl became convinced he was automatically going to hit into a double play. So when Dauer did hit into another double play, Earl would put his head in his hands and mumble, "Why can't he pop up once in a while?" Translation: Why can't he do something bad that's not the same as the bad thing he's been doing, or, in this case, make one out instead of two? Be half as bad. The Positive of being *less* Negative.

Then there's the total, give-up, 100 percent Negative. When the other team hits a fly ball into shallow right and our first baseman and second baseman and right fielder all go for the ball but nobody gets there. Earl shakes his head and yells, "Another ball lost in the Bermuda Triangle!" That'll get the fielders there faster next time. Call it a lost cause and who knows how hard a guy will try? Make people feel like idiots. Always a persuasive technique.

It's what he used on Don Hood when he came up in '74. He's getting his first pitching start, it's against the Yankees, we're in the middle of a pennant race, and we're behind, 2–0. He goes to back up home on a play so he's near Earl and Earl says, "You're fucking choking!" For encouragement.

And encouragement, especially of pitchers, was Earl's specialty. That is, Positive-Negative encouragement. Earl was going over the lineup with me before a game with Milwaukee and he says, "Okay, there's Yount. Shit, there's nothing you can throw past Yount. Cecil Cooper. He's eighteen for twenty. No hope there. Larry Hisle, he's really been hitting. . . ." And he walks away!

But, just in case I have a shred of hope left, he's not done. Earl stops in front of the other guys and says, "We're gonna need a bunch of runs to beat these guys." Boy, I know I was encouraged.

Elrod Hendricks, our catcher during some great years, had the unenviable job of picking pitchers up after Earl "encouraged" them into pathological depression. Everybody (okay, almost everybody) in baseball knows, there are two words you should never use with a pitcher. *Don't* and *can't*.

So, Elrod said he'd go to the mound and Earl would be saying to the pitcher, "Well, you don't have Palmer's fastball. You don't have Cuellar's curveball. You sure don't have a slider. And you can't throw this guy a change-up." Then he'd walk off the mound. Leaving the pitcher with his spirits lifted. Motivated. And leaving Hendricks with a "don't-can't" basket case.

Now if the Positive-Negative is good for ballplayers, imagine how effective it could be with umpires. Exactly Earl's thinking. He called them names and yelled at them, turned his hat backward so he could yell even closer to their faces, kicked dirt on them, yelled some more, and thought all that would make them try harder. High-level psychology at work.

He attacked, abused, berated, bedeviled, and be-totally-pissed-off Ron Luciano. He protested any game Luciano umped.

He second-, third-, and fourth-guessed every call Steve Palermo ever made in his whole career, which, by the law of averages seems a little harsh, since he had a one out of two chance on every pitch.

And, when Earl was wired with a microphone by the TV network, he screamed at Bill Haller something about how he, Earl, shouldn't be treated this way because "I'm going to the Hall of Fame." And Haller came back with, "For what, fucking up the '79 World Series?" See, the Negative-Positive was working its magic right there. Haller was trying real hard to be better.

Once, though, I recall Earl being nice to an umpire, in a backhanded, perverse kind of way. We were playing a doubleheader against the Senators. It was the same doubleheader when we struck out Frank Howard, "Big Hondo," eight times, four times in my game and four times in the second game, and he went back to the dugout and calmly broke a bat over his own knee.

But what makes the day even more memorable was Earl being civil to an umpire. What happened was that Ken McMullen, the Senators third baseman, hit a shot to left field and Don Buford races in and spears this sinking line drive, knee high. Emmett Ashford, the umpire, comes running in and calls McMullen safe.

Earl, instead of going from zero to insane in four seconds, calmly says to Ashford, "Can you change your call? Just ask the other umpires, because I understand you couldn't see it where you were running from." Amazingly, Ashford asks the other umpires and they say that Buford caught the ball and Ashford calls McMullen out.

I'm pretty happy about it because I'm pitching in the ninth inning and it protects my 2–0 lead. But here comes Ted Williams, who's managing the Senators, and he sees it different. He hollers, "You son of a bitch, how can you make that fucking call?"

And I'm thinking, "Wow, so this is Ted Williams. I've never met him." Interesting how you first encounter legends.

But Ashford stuck to his call, or his recall. And Earl was very complimentary to him in the papers. It never seemed to dawn on Earl that he had not yelled and screamed and acted like a straitjacket model and Ashford had cooperated. He didn't act negative. He acted positive. But it didn't stick.

Otherwise Earl might not have gotten out-of-his-beet-red-skull-capital-f Furious with Marty Springstead in Cleveland one day. And he wouldn't have stormed back to the dugout and gotten Ray Miller to get him a rule book and he wouldn't have stormed back out to home plate with the rule book in his back pocket. And when Springstead warned him, "Don't take that book out or you're outta here," Earl wouldn't have pulled it out, pointing at the page where the rule was that Earl was sure Springstead was ignoring and Earl definitely wouldn't have said, "I guess we're not playing by the rules anymore so we won't need this." And he definitely wouldn't have torn the rule book to pieces.

But he did. He did all those things.

Springstead only did one thing. He threw Earl out.

A reporter asked Earl for his opinion of Springstead, and Earl said, "He's a terrific guy." Pause. "He's just not a very good umpire." Earl thought an honest assessment like that was bound to motivate Springstead. Make him try harder.

But, oddly enough, after the season was over and Springstead was on the speech circuit, his comment on Earl was, they ought to do a Timex watch ad—one of those "takes a licking and keeps on ticking" commercials—by tying a watch to Earl's tongue.

Earl's unique motivational approach didn't seem to take with Marty Springstead. Oh, he did get good enough to become the director of umpires for the entire American League, which he still is today. But he never got good enough for Earl. In spite of all that free Positive-Negative input Earl offered.

The name-calling, the tantrums, the yelling. Some guys just don't want to be helped. Even swearing at them doesn't work.

Of course, Earl insisted he never used four-letter words. He claimed he'd go head to head with an umpire and call him a "no-good rock-sucker!" and the umpire would eject him. Over that. An innocent expression of dissatisfaction meant to infuse the recipient with the desire for self-improvement.

Tell him he stinks so he'll try *not* to stink. *Not* to make bad calls. *Not* to give up walks. *Not* to strike out. *Not* to lose the ball in the sun. *Not* to be stupid. *Not* to be bad.

The Positive-Negative. Why hasn't the UN discovered this stuff?

I Was Like the Son Earl Weaver Never Had. His Real Sons Were Easy to Get Along With.

I was unhappy in 1979. I was upset. I was annoyed. I was miserable. And I was highly contagious. I got a lot of other people unhappy, upset, annoyed, and miserable.

I'd had a good year in '77 and a really good year in '78, and now we were in first place in '79 but I was being paid based on a contract I signed *before*. Before players played out their options. Before owners had to pay what players were worth. Before free agency. Which turned out to be anything but free for owners.

Before was officially over and *after* was here. The money that owners had sworn for years before on a stack of checkbooks just wasn't there, was there after all. In fact, the owners must've been constipated with money because after that, it flowed like sewage. They gave it to great players, good players, and players they were afraid might someday turn out to be two shades above mediocre.

Bert Blyleven wins seventeen games and gets $450,000. Vida Blue has a deal that gets him up to $500,000 with deferred payments into the next century! I'd won two hundred games, but twenty-one pitchers in baseball were making more than me. I'm watching other guys cash checks that should've had my name on them! Call it petty. Call it envy. Call it jealousy. Call it shallow . . . hey, enough. It wasn't pretty. I admit it. (Of course now, almost twenty years later, I'm over it . . . or I will be soon.)

Sometimes, maybe daily, I let my true feelings show to newspaper reporters who, maybe daily, printed it, and some of the guys on the team, including Earl, got sick and tired of reading the same story, but I didn't care because I was angry and wanted to be paid more. Hey, I already admitted I wasn't proud of it.

So, I gave this interview to the *St. Paul Pioneer Press*. I may have mentioned in passing that I thought my contract was a tad less generous than it could be. I might have offered some "constructive criticism" to the Orioles management.

Okay, I bitched for two straight hours, and the guy printed it word for word. Including my inspired closer, "I'm going to aggravate them until they trade me."

The next day, Sunday, June 17, in Minneapolis, that article was pinned to my locker with a note. "Happy Father's Day. Now grow up." Unsigned. Anonymous. From Earl.

Weaver could hardly wait for the reporters. "Yeah, you could say I'm aggravated! It's the same thing, day after day, city after city. . . . He's right, he's underpaid. But it's not my fault or Hank Peters's fault or Jerry Hoffberger's fault. It's Jim Palmer's fault. He's worth a million dollars *when he's pitching* but he signed for $260,000."

The "when he's pitching" part was a shot at me because I had missed five starts in a row with arm trouble and had gone back to see Dr. Kerlan in L.A. for treatment. People were saying, pain or no pain, I should be pitching since we were in a pennant race and they were saying I was just refusing to pitch as a ploy to get traded.

Earl talked to every reporter in the clubhouse. He was steamed. "See this head of gray hair? Every one of them belongs to Jim Palmer." He never said he put the note on my locker, but he said everything but. "It's time for him to act his age!"

I guess he was right. I was thirty-three with two kids. I should have acted my age. I shouldn't have bitched to the papers about getting screwed by the owners.

I should have kicked dirt on their shoes and turned my hat backward and screamed obscenities in their faces. I should have acted my age like Earl did.

Anyway, like always, we both got over it. The team played great. I pitched better. We won the pennant.

Mike Flanagan had called it, "Just another dull Sunday afternoon." But it wasn't. It was Father's Day. Two grown men acting like kids.

Hey, Earl, It Was Me Who Said Those Nice Things to the Writer from *Time* Magazine

It's the '79 season and a lot of the guys are down on Earl because either they're not playing so he isn't talking to them or they *are* playing so he *is* talking to them, which is way worse, and Earl has just left his infamous and sentimental Father's Day message on my locker, "Grow up!" so we're pretty tight . . . but, in the meantime, the team is winning and we're in the pennant race so *Time* magazine decides to do a cover story on him.

This writer follows us around for two weeks. He hears the bitching and cursing and he witnesses the ranting and the rages and he ducks a couple of thrown chairs and remember, this is Earl in a good mood because we're winning. And guys like Belanger are filling this reporter with serious ear poison and other guys are talking about how Earl's ex-wives like him about as much as umpires do and Steve Stone says Earl has a Napoleon complex. (I thought Napoleon had an Earl complex. And Napoleon's record wasn't nearly as good.)

So somebody *has* to say something good about Earl. I elect

me. Probably the guy least expected to do it given our history of mutual admiration. But I figure it's for the good of the team. I mean, this writer is doing a great big article for, in Earl's words, *"Time* fuckin' magazine," and everybody in the United States is going to read the story and then we're all going to have to live with "it." "It" being Earl. So, "it" better come out looking good. Or as good as "it" can. (See, I really don't mind saying nice things about Earl . . . as long as I don't have to do it in front of him.)

I tell this reporter that Earl was put on earth only to win. I tell him to overlook Earl's quirks and fits and language because the man is demonically driven to win; he is obsessed and possessed by winning; he breathes in and out to win . . . all this melodramatic stuff which all happens to be true. I mean, it's the only excuse there is for a guy acting like a homicidal maniac every summer.

I figure I have saved Earl from embarrassment. And, in the process, I've saved the team from having to live with a pissed-off, offended Earl who would be beyond all the Earls they've ever experienced, Hyper-Earl, Earl to the tenth power, Earl-enstein!

What I don't realize is, he didn't need any help. Writers love Earl. They love his oddities. They love his double . . . and triple . . . negatives. They love his addiction to fried chicken and his hatred of umpires. They love to write about him. And they love to please him.

He'd pin up their articles and grade them. The guy from the *Globe* gets a B+ and he's all smiles. The guy from the *Sun* gets a C- and he stays after class to ask Earl what he did wrong. He had these guys in his pocket. Because he understood their jobs depended on him. He had the information. He was quotable. He was the lifeblood. A guy like me, they only talked to every fourth day. Him they needed every single day. No Earl, no story. He had them right where he wanted them. If opposing teams were made of reporters, Earl wouldn't have needed nine guys to win. He'd be 162–0 every year.

The *Time* article was just like a story in the *Plain Dealer* or the *Free Press* or the *Daily News,* only longer and more complimentary. The writer got an A. Earl came out smelling like a rose.

Unfortunately for Earl but fortunately for the world, he got bumped off the cover of *Time* by Anwar Sadat and Menachem Begin. It is not true, by the way, that when it happened, Earl asked who they played for.

Why Pitch a Cy Young Winner When You Can Pitch an Old Guy with a Sore Arm?

If garlic keeps vampires away, I was pretty much Dracula-free in 1979. Actually, it wasn't garlic, it just smelled like garlic. There's this anti-inflammatory stuff called DMSO that you apply topically, and except for the anchovies, lettuce, and croutons, you could pass for a Caesar salad.

I'm pitching, and keeping vampires and opposing batters at a safe distance in Cleveland, pitching longer and better than I have in a while, with a 13–0 lead going into the seventh inning. Then I give up a couple of runs, a guy lines one up the middle, uncomfortably close to my forehead, and Earl comes to take me out.

He always wanted to go to the top of the mound in any stadium, but especially in Cleveland, at the old Municipal Stadium, where the mound was, despite whatever the rules claim, just a little lower than Mount Kilimanjaro. But I stayed on the mound, which is to say, several thousand feet above sea level and Earl.

I hand him the ball and he says, "Don't ever put the fucking ball in my face again!"

I say, "Earl, it was waist high when it left my hand."

He launches into this tirade. "You called me a drunk in the *Washington Post*."

Suddenly, I get it. The week before, Tom Boswell had called to ask me about my arm and about the California Angels, who we were going to face in the playoffs, who happened to have the most powerful offense in baseball that year, plus Nolan Ryan pitching . . . and about whether Earl was drinking a lot.

I said, "Tom, I'm not going to comment on that. You go on a couple of road trips and judge for yourself. All I know is that we're having a great year."

Tom evidently took some license and supposedly suggested that Earl was the official poster boy for Smirnoff vodka.

So Earl is fuming. But he wouldn't let anything get in the way of winning. He wouldn't bring it up before the game or while I was pitching; only when he knew I was headed for the showers.

The game's over, I go to wash off the DMSO (and brush my teeth and gargle and eat breath mints) and eventually ice my arm, and Earl comes flying over to me and says, "Come into my office!"

I figure he's still steaming over the drinking story, so I say, "Earl, I don't know what you were talking about with the *Post* story. I'd never take a cheap shot at you and I'm not going to comment on whether you were drinking and . . ."

Earl says, "Okay, fine. You're pitching the first game of the playoffs." He's done with the drinking thing and he's back to winning. Over. Done. Now about baseball and real life-sustaining issues.

He says, "How do you feel?"

I feel fine.

"Good," he says, "because you're pitching Game 1."

I'm still about a chapter behind but I'm catching up. And this is, to me, a monumentally blockheaded idea.

In 1979, Mike Flanagan won twenty-three games with a 3.08 ERA and he's on his way to winning the Cy Young Award. And I'm nursing a sore elbow . . . and death breath.

I know why Earl wants to pitch me. Experience. I've pitched in the World Series, and All-Star games, and playoffs, and had a good record under pressure. But I know, if I pitch the first game, since it's a three-out-of-five series, I'll have to pitch the fifth game, and I may not be any good for Game 5 the way my arm and elbow are feeling. If there is a Game 5, it'll be a must-win, and the best guy for that is Flanagan, not me.

Anyone can see, me pitching Game 1 is clearly a bad idea. Anyone but Earl.

I say, "Earl, this is very flattering, but for the good of the team, Flanagan should pitch Game 1."

Earl says, "No, you're pitching the first game."

I say, "I'll pitch any game *except* game one."

And he says a little louder . . . and I say a lot louder . . . and he says even louder . . . and the door to his office opens and there's Ed Keating, who represented me at the time and used to be with Mark McCormack and used to represent Earl. Ed says, with a big shit-eating grin, "You guys need a referee?"

Earl replies politely, "No, get the fuck outa here." And Ed gets the fuck out of there.

Earl "explains" it to me. "Either you pitch the first game or you go on the disabled list."

I wasn't disabled. For the first time all year, I didn't hurt anywhere. (If you don't count what my garlic breath did to other people.) I say, "Obviously we can't talk about this rationally. I'm going to have to go to Hank Peters [who Earl knows I don't get along with, so I must be serious] and see what he says."

Very maturely, Earl responds, "Oh yeah?"

We come back to Baltimore and clinch the division and the next day I'm at the ballpark. We had celebrated pretty good the night before, which, Mr. Boswell of the *Post,* is not to suggest anything about anyone drinking. It's just a fact because we had won.

This, I calculate shrewdly, is the perfect time to have a calm, sensible discussion on the topic of who pitches the first game of the playoffs. I open, "Well, Earl, now can we talk about Flanagan . . . ?"

He screams, "You fucking quit on me again. You quit! Did you hear that? Quit!" And he's got an audience of Ray Miller, the pitching coach, and Jimmy Frey, the first-base coach, and some players and I think the only one missing was the pope.

I turn to go to the training room and say, "Earl, I want to talk to Hank Peters."

As I go to close the door, Earl sticks his foot in the door and for a moment, time stops. Do I want to break his foot in the door? I am furious with him. Do I want to just slam it and snap that annoying little appendage in two? One quick, clean motion and he could be *limping* out to the mound for the next couple of weeks. Right then a newspaper headline types out across my mind: PALMER BREAKS WEAVER'S FOOT.

It was sort of a battle between the little devil on your one shoulder and the little angel on your other shoulder.

"Do it! Do it!"

"No-no-no, don't do it."

"Go ahead, you know you want to!"

"But you know you shouldn't."

Finally, the devil lost. I opened the door, muttered something about having to stoop to his level, and then actually stooped to his level, and went into the training room.

We did go see Peters and he sided with Earl. No surprise. I knew it. Earl knew that I knew it. Earl was the manager.

I pitched the first game and gave up three runs in nine innings. We were tied at 3–3, and in the bottom of the tenth John Lowenstein hit an opposite-field home run and we won.

We won the next one in Baltimore. Flanagan pitched and we had a six- or seven-run lead when Don Stanhouse came in and then we almost lost it but pulled it out 11–10 while Earl nearly had several heart attacks.

Then we lost the third one in Anaheim in the last inning.

Now I'm getting nervous about my Game 5 prediction.

But Scotty McGregor pitches a 4–0 shutout, we win the fourth game, and there is no fifth game.

I was convinced I was right and we were just lucky and good enough to win in four. But if there was a fifth game, a big game, Earl figured he'd pitch *Experience* in a big game. Earl knew, when you're one win away from a trip to the World Series, even if *Experience's* arm hurts, he'll just pitch and then have three and a half months to heal his experienced arm.

Earl had a plan, not just a rock-hard head. But he had a hard head, too. An experienced hard head.

1980 and '81
Lousy, Followed by Mediocre

We were tough. We were scrappy. We fought to the bitter end. And we were pretty tough on the field, too. But it was one of those times when nothing worked. Even Earl couldn't change it.

By 1980, the Orioles dynasty was aging.

Earl Weaver had put together contenders for almost a dozen years. He had found the fielders, pitchers, and batters to keep the Birds in the thick of the pennant race season after season.

And he had counted on the durability of Jim Palmer's sore but sure arm. Time took its toll.

Jim suffered more aches and pains, had to leave more games, and simply couldn't bounce back as fast after injuries.

His career off the field thrived, but on the field it was ailing.

The years 1980 and 1981 were healing times for Palmer and rebuilding times for the Orioles.

Hypochondria

Throughout my career, some people have accused me of being a hypochondriac. I'd like to set the record straight. People who think I complain about imaginary illnesses give me a sort of sharp, shooting pain that seems to reverberate through my upper shoulder muscles causing a convulsing spasm that may not show up on diagnostic tests but was verified by a native root therapist in the upper Andes.

My pains were real. And there weren't all that many of them, anyway. Let's see. . . .

I had a bad back starting, well, almost when I started in 1965. (I might have had it in high school, too, but I don't think that counts.)

Nineteen sixty-five was also the year I got a sore arm and started taking cortisone, which helped for a while but it actually caused some soreness of its own. Cortisone side-effect syndrome.

And all right, so I did soak in the whirlpool so much the other guys named it the SS *Palmer*.

Then, in 1966, I won that World Series game but thank God I didn't have to pitch a second game since I had hurt my neck and arm painting my house. Which definitely had something to do with me being sent down to Triple A the next year and then to Puerto Rico. By the time I got there I had come across Indocin from this drug salesman I met at the Bullets basketball game. He got it out of his car at halftime so I don't think that should count as a doctor's appointment.

But the Indocin helped my sore arm more than those doctors at Sinai Hospital in Baltimore. I guess I had seen all of them, by then. And this was way before sports medicine, a specialty that some people give me the credit for starting.

Sure, I did take a few medications and treatments along the way. Anti-inflammatories. Aloe vera. Indocin. DMSO. Medrol packs. Horse pain killers. Pills. Capsules. Creams. Gels. Pastes. Wraps. Spells. Chants. Curses. Animal feces. Okay, so they weren't all covered by insurance.

But it still hurt, my arm did. And my shoulder, by now. Which was why I had to drop in on a few docs when we were on the road in Chicago and Boston (great medical city!) and Detroit, where I saw Dr. Russell Wright, the Olympic weight-lifting physician.

And I should mention, Dr. Arthur Pappas, who was the team doctor and part-owner of the Red Sox. Also, a guy in Omaha who trained with Sumos and some distant relative of the Mayo brothers from Minneapolis and the acupuncturist from Scottsdale and the guy at the Cleveland Clinic and an ex-Yankee doc who, I say, should never have lost his medical license. And this man from India whose name I can't remember. Or maybe it was Turkey.

Of course, there was Dr. Chick Silberstein of the Orioles, who worked closely with our trainer, Ralph Salvon. And Ralph could attest to the fact that I was in pain since I drove and he ate his way to Florida for spring training every year. I can't tell you how many times my arm was too sore to reach into the backseat for his Cheetos, Doritos, Twinkies, Ding Dongs, or those little hot dogs in the tin can. But Ralph knew exactly how many times.

All the experts saw me. You know, just checking me over. Looking for that pain in my arm-shoulder-back-neck area. Most of these experts never saw it or felt it or found it on X-rays. They must have just missed it because it was really there.

For instance, there was the elbow inflammation—boy, that was painful!—lifting and lowering things, so I stopped for a year or so. It was Harry Brecheen, one of our pitching coaches, who said, "Don't do anything. I picked up a suitcase once and it ruined 1954 for me." That's why I took up tennis left-handed so I wouldn't put any more strain on my right arm. Except picking up the balls. Once I grabbed two at once . . . well, it wasn't pretty.

But back to my doctor collection. There was Dr. Charles Virgin Sr. of the Miami Dolphins (there was also his son, Virgin Jr., who basically agreed with the older Virgin's diagnosis) and Sr. said, when he checked me out, "Your career is over." But I kept pitching.

The credit for that goes to Dr. Kerlan, who I had seen a while ago in L.A. and who was the one who figured out what was wrong with me, which wasn't what Hank Bauer thought when he said, "It's all in your head," to which I said, "If it's in my head, how come when I throw, my arm hurts and not my head?"

Dr. Kerlan, who was *not* a shrink, got me straightened out. He said it was biceptal tendonitis. See? It has a name so it must be real. And with these stretches and medication and rest, I kept pitching. In spite of what Dr. Virgin said.

And after that, except for one of my legs being a third of an inch shorter than the other causing lumbar contractions and the need for lifts which hurt my arches and my floating sixth vertebrae resulting in constant shoulder and neck discomfort and a pinched nerve shooting hot spots up the back of my head and tight hamstrings so I couldn't walk and, of course, the rotator cuff thing so I couldn't throw fastballs as fast, well otherwise, I was pretty much problem-free.

The way I see it, I didn't complain about a lot of things. I complained about one thing. Pain. I went to the doctor like anybody would. All right, I went to many doctors. When the movie *Dr. Zhivago* came out, Steve Stone, another O's pitcher, said I went to see it because I thought it was about an elbow specialist.

Maybe I was a hypochondriac. Maybe I exaggerated. Maybe not. One guy who disagreed with me on everything else never doubted me for a second when I said I was hurt. Earl. If I said I was hurt, I was hurt. Although he did say, the Chinese had the Year of the Rat or the Year of the Tiger, and with me, he had the Year of the Ulna Nerve. (Hey, I almost forgot that one.)

But I can tell you the best part of being a baseball pitcher. It's the day after the season ends. You wake up in the morning and it doesn't matter how your arm feels.

Enough on this. I've got a cramp in my hand from writing.

Method Acting

By 1980, I had been doing the Jockey underwear advertising for a little while and, it may be hard to imagine now but back then, it caused a minor sexual stir. At one point, my poster was going faster than Cheryl Tiegs's. A baseball player in his underwear. Pretty racy.

This was before those Calvin Klein ads where you can't tell whose arm is wrapped around whose thigh or what's being done to whom with which thing. Or the Guess ads that are sort of like triple X, black socks, porno movies only dirtier.

I just took my shirt off and sat there. In my white Jockey shorts. And later my blue ones and my green ones and my black ones. Whoa!

The idea was to get more and more women, who bought most of the men's underwear, to see this pitcher that their husband watched on TV, sitting around in his colored underwear and say, "Hey, my old man, Gus, would look okay in a pair of fire-engine red shorts, too." Convince America that these colored Jockey shorts are for the average guy, the everyman, jock or fan, big or small, tall, or short. Everybody.

So the inevitable was unavoidable. Get another guy, say, a real regular guy, to be in an ad with me. A guy not like me at all. Opposite to me. Now who could that be?

That's how Earl Weaver and I happened to spend the better (or worse) part of a day in a film studio in New York one

February day. The idea was that I'd be in the locker room wearing my colored underwear, naturally with no shirt on in a shameless appeal to the smutty minds of Midwestern housewives, and Earl would come in wearing a colored T-shirt (and God knows what under his pants since he was more modest.) See, big league ballplayers wear Jockey's latest and so does a big league manager who's even older and more mature, not to mention shorter and gray-haired.

And it went off without a hitch. Except Earl kept saying "made" when he was supposed to say "make," and no matter how much I corrected him, he kept getting it wrong . . . just like when I tried to help him on the field.

And I did suggest to the film crew that they move around to some better positions. A little deeper, closer to the line, over here, over there. The director paid no attention to me. I think Earl told him to just ignore me and smile and eventually I'd make my "pitch." Which I did.

The end of the ad was supposed to have Earl getting mad at me like we were famous for. Now, up to this point, like I said, he got his lines wrong and, in my more experienced opinion, he was a little nervous and camera shy. I was sort of carrying him.

Then comes the get-mad-at-Palmer part. Earl is going to have to pretend to really be mad. Even though this is just a commercial. So the director says, "Action!" and Earl starts hollering his head off at me, turning beet red, yelling right in my face, going Earl-nuts! It was so real.

Funny how easy that part came to him. I didn't have to help him at all.

World Peace

The infamous DeCinces-Palmer Feud wasn't my fault or Doug DeCinces's fault. It was Brooks Robinson's fault. Even though Brooks wasn't playing that day, wasn't even playing that season, and, in fact, had retired altogether four years before, it was definitely his fault.

If Brooks hadn't been the best third baseman of all time, the rest of the Orioles wouldn't have taken it for granted that any ball hit anywhere within the same county as Brooks would be judged perfectly, fielded perfectly, and thrown perfectly, nailing (perfectly) what seemed like every single opposing batter. And then we wouldn't have been disappointed in *any* other third baseman who judged, fielded, threw, or nailed any less than perfectly . . . which means basically, *all* other third basemen ever, including Doug DeCinces.

We were spoiled. Especially me. Some pitchers get a lot of guys out on strikeouts. Pitchers like Nolan Ryan. Some pitchers get a lot of guys out by getting them to hit ground balls, line drives, and pop-ups, that get turned into outs by fielders. Pitchers like me.

I need fielders. I want to win more than anything. When they don't do what I think they can do, it bothers me a little. Okay, a lot. And I show it in subtle ways like waving my arms around, muttering, kicking the mound, shaking my head, and waving my arms around some more. I didn't say I act mature; I said I want to win.

I thought DeCinces could have/should have caught Alan Trammell's shot down the third base line and stopped the Tigers rally. I thought he shouldn't backhand balls down the line. I thought he should forget about all the broken noses he got in the minors and throw himself in front of the ball. I thought he should have stopped the ball and thrown Trammell out at first. I thought that's what Brooks would've done.

And I thought Earl Weaver should've been telling DeCinces to do it. It was Earl's job. Just like it was Earl's job to tell Pat Kelly to stop preaching to everybody about the power of the Lord when he was supposed to be playing the outfield and learn to play the outfield better . . . which, by the way, would've been a way more convincing testimony to the power of the Lord.

But Earl didn't tell DeCinces to stop backhanding hits down the line and he didn't tell Kelly to stop worrying about the miracle of being born again and worry more about the miracle of us winning again. Earl said they're major leaguers. It wasn't his place to offer them advice on how to play their positions. This admirable restraint evidently didn't extend to pitchers, who Earl thought needed all the advice an expert like himself, who never *was* a pitcher, never *caught* a pitcher, and never *hit* a pitcher, could offer.

Maybe I overdid my display of disappointment at DeCinces's handling of Trammell's hit. Maybe that's why DeCinces told the *Baltimore Sun* reporter, "He was cussing me out and throwing his hands in the air. I'm upset that he has to make comments about a play that was a hit all the way." (Okay, the scorer called it a double, but to me it was an error.)

Maybe that's why I told the reporter, "Those balls have to be caught. Doug is reluctant to get in front of a ball. I know that. I understand that he's broken his nose so many times. But he doesn't have to get into a dialogue in the paper about it."

And maybe that's why DeCinces told the reporter, "I'd like to know where Jim Palmer gets off criticizing others. Ask anybody—they're all sick of it. We're a twenty-four–man team—and one prima donna. He thinks it's always someone else's fault."

Which may be why I told the reporter, "I don't know why Doug DeCinces has to say these things in public . . . unless he feels guilty."

And that could be what made DeCinces tell the reporter, "I don't want him destroying what we have on the club. Everybody's going to make physical errors, and we don't throw our hands in the air every time someone hits a homer off Jim."

Maybe all that he-said-I-said stuff is what feuds are made

of. Plus a little fuel from some sportswriters about me coming out of the game in the second inning with a sore neck and saying it was connected to the third base incident. And then the writers go to Earl and stir the pot a little more because it does sell papers. So how did Earl, a guy who wants to win as much or more than me, handle it? A guy who's been called a "hothead" and then said "thank you." How did that guy handle it?

FEUD EASED BY WEAVER. That headline on the sports page of the *Sun* on Friday, June 5, 1981, says it all. He handled it the same way he handled DeCinces's backhanding-balls-down-the-line style and Kelly's God-in-the-outfield situation. He underhandled it. And, hear me Earl, you were right.

When those feud-fueling, pot-stirring, paper-peddling reporters descended on Earl, he shrugged and said, "I see no cause for concern. The third baseman wants the pitcher to do a little better and the pitcher wants the third baseman to do a little better. I hope we can all do better and kiss and make up." Almost like it was motivating and positive and what all good teams do. Brilliant.

When the writers pushed harder on the connection with my neck injury, he just said he wouldn't want me to play when I'm hurt and that's why you have other pitchers on your staff.

And when DeCinces and I wouldn't let the thing die a quiet death and the writers kept trying to rile Earl, he just spit, took a drag of his cigarette, shrugged again, and made it all part of the great game of baseball. "I don't worry about things like that. Some guys get angry and do better. So, how can you lose? The judge gave me custody of both of them."

Finish with a laugh. The reporters loved him. And the feud fizzled. Kissinger couldn't have done it better. Earl didn't put us in a room and force us to make up. He let us play baseball. Our way. He talked to the papers. His way.

Of course, he wouldn't have had to do anything if it hadn't have been for Brooks Robinson and his habit of playing third base perfectly. It's pretty obvious, you have to blame Brooks.

The Earl and Me Feud of '81

My feud with Earl in '81 was pretty much like my feuds with Earl in '75 or '78 or '79 except, since it was '81, I was older. I didn't pitch like I was in my twenties for a very simple reason. I wasn't. And every day my body reminded me.

Not to mention opposing batters. They love to remind you. They love to remind you when they hit your fastball and show you it's not so fast coming in but plenty fast going out. Or they wait and wait and wait for your curve to break and then straighten the curve out, right past your head. So you have to pitch smarter. You have to use your years and your gut and your head to outthink 'em. When it works, everybody thinks you can go on forever (except you and your manager), but when it doesn't, everybody starts thinking it's over (including you and your manager).

And the one thing you need more than anything is breaks. You need grounders that turn into double plays. You need heroic catches on foul balls that are practically in the third row of the lower deck. You need sure home run shots that get blown back into the field by winds that are blowing your way. You need a team that fields like a Hoover Upright and hits like a twelve-year-old arcade jockey on a Nintendo game.

But when fate turns on you and takes an easy, long fly and carries it the last ten feet over the short left field fence in Seattle for a home run and maybe, just maybe, there wasn't as much on that last pitch as you wanted so the batter got a bigger piece of it, when that happens, you feel like Shit, with a capital *S*.

And Earl comes out to the mound and what should have been a regular old "What the fuck is going on, Jimmy?"—"Get outta here and just let me finish 'em off, Earl" conversation turns into a Battle of the Maniacs to see who's the bigger maniac, ending with the one Maniac-in-Charge sending the Pitching Maniac to the showers. He's yelling on the mound and I'm yelling on the mound and we're both yelling off the mound and on the way to the dugout and after we're in the dugout and inside each of our heads with *shoulda-saids* for the next three innings.

But the game is finally over and I can go to my locker that used to be near Earl's office but that I've moved as far away as possible. So Earl sits in his office and blows off steam with reporters who then trot down to my faraway locker to get my response to his steam and then trot back up to his office to get his response to my response and ad nauseam, or at least I want to puke.

A couple of days after the easy, long fly that grew up to be a free home run in Seattle, Tom Boswell of the *Washington Post* asks about how far away I've moved my locker and Earl says, "I don't care if he dresses in the visitors' clubhouse. When I want him, I'll just send Ray Miller [the pitching coach] over to drag him back by his diaper."

Evidently, Earl thinks that even though I'm getting older, I'm not acting like it. Me?! What about him?! He did it first! I just did it back!

Now I get to have my response to his response to my response. I tell Boswell something on the order of, "Listen, don't you think I know what you're doing? You run in there, you get something, you run out here, you get something, and you go back in there. Since you're going back to talk to Earl, tell him this. If he's so insecure that I can't tell him how I feel, after pitching for him for the last twelve years, he's got a major problem!"

And Boswell does. He runs back into Earl's office and tells him what I said about what he said. And the *Post* prints the back and forth and the Feud of '81 is on and the fans and readers are happy.

Except one reader. Earl Weaver. I don't realize it but I have hit a nerve. No, make that a whole nerve mine. A school of nerves. A nerve nation. Earl is seething, burning, frying, molten-hot, berserk! But I don't know it yet. However, "yet" is only a few hours away.

I pitch the next day against the Angels. I pitch shitty against the Angels.

After the shitty game, Earl and his wife, Marianne, go out for dinner and a few cocktails. And he has approximately the same number of drinks as I had strikeouts, which is, statistically, not a high number of strikeouts but is, statistically, a fair number of drinks. At this point, he's pretty much nothing but exposed nerve-endings. And, to everybody or nobody in particular in the restaurant, Hersh's Orchard Inn, he says, "You can call me a mother-fucker. You can call me a cocksucker. But don't . . . don't you ever call me insecure!"

Finally, it's time to go home and, as usual, Marianne is driving. She sees that a cop has pulled somebody over on the highway and she pulls over and just stops. She decides she shouldn't be driving and she gets out to walk back to the restaurant.

Now Earl is sitting in the car, not driving or planning to drive, just sitting there, when the cop wanders over to him. He leans in and says, "Sir, are you okay?"

And Earl doesn't answer.

The cop says, "Do you know your name?"

And Earl doesn't answer.

The cop says, "Do you know where you are?"

No answer.

The cop says, "Sir, do you have a physical disability?"

Earl says, "Yeah, Jim Palmer."

So it's safe to say this word bothered him. "Insecure." Call it a hunch. For one word to get to someone that much, the guy would have to be very . . . uh . . . unsure . . . not self-confident . . . what's the word I'm searching for?

Like I said, I'm older now. So what I lack in speed and control, I make up for in tactics. Like picking just the right word to send Earl over the edge.

The More Things Change

"This strike is killing the game."

"The owners are trying to teach the players a lesson."

"I really don't see us playing the rest of the year."

"Nobody is acting in the best interests of the game. I don't feel sorry for either side. I feel sorry for the fans. . . ."

Sounds like I'm talking about the baseball strike of 1994. But I wasn't. That's what I said about the strike of 1981. Nothing changed in the next thirteen years. The issue in '94 was the issue of '81. Money. Plain old money. Stacks of money. Money with a string of zeroes after it. Oh, both sides gave it lots of other names, like compensation, player pools, offsets, free market, and various thesaurusized substitutes for one green word, *m-o-n-e-y*.

Ever since free agency, the owners wanted a "get-back," as in, "we gotta get back some of the money we're paying these guys." They wanted an end to binding arbitration where the player picks a salary number (a high one) and the owners pick a number (yes, a low one) and the arbitrator has to choose one number or the other and nothing in between. So, since the owners kept paying more and more to mediocre players, the averages kept going up and the arbitrators looked at the averages and usually went with the player's number, which raised the average some more.

It was the Ed Farmer factor. Ed was a relief pitcher who had been with lots of teams in the major and minor leagues. He played on the Orioles in '77. Ed was okay. He was making $70,000 after fifteen years in the game. Okay money for an okay player.

Then Ed went to arbitration. He asked for $495,000. Why $495,000? Who knows? Maybe he didn't want to appear greedy and ask for a full half million. Maybe he thought it looked like a sale price . . . like *"$4.95, this week only."*

The White Sox offered $300,000, probably thinking they were being extravagant. The arbitrator gave him the whole $495,000. Boom! The averages keep climbing.

And that's not to say I sided with the owners. They were still dreaming of the past, back when they had total South American dictator control over the game, the players, the coaches, the concessions, the parking, the bathrooms, everything but the weather, and they were pissed off about that.

The owners were dying for a return to the good old days. Like my first year in the game. I'm making $500 a month in Aberdeen, South Dakota. I went 11–3 and we had this great team managed by Cal Ripken Sr. We finished somewhere around 81–31.

So the Orioles tell me they want me to go to Clearwater for some more work and I go there and I'm 5–1, so I end up 16–4.

I'm feeling pretty good when I go back to Scottsdale, that is, until my first contract arrives and it's for . . . $500 a month . . . again. Even as a kid I know this isn't right. So I send it back. They send another one: $500 a month. I send it back. They send another one: $500 a month again.

Now I don't know what to do, so I ask Steve Caria, who I'd known since Babe Ruth League days. We were the top two pitching prospects in the Orioles organization. He tells me to tear up the contract and send it back.

And I do. But the Orioles keep sending back the same contract. Now it's getting to the point where on $500 a month I can't afford any more postage, but I'm pretty sure the Orioles have an unlimited number of stamps.

Steve tells me to tell the Orioles my wife is pregnant. I say, "She's not pregnant."

He looks at me like "What does that have to do with it?"

I write a letter to Lee MacPhail, the GM. "Dear Lee, my wife is pregnant."

A contract arrives for $600 a month. A $100 raise, not because I pitched well but because I'm pleading for a baby. That was the paternalistic, all-powerful, we-know-what's-good-for-you, attitude of management. *"See, we do have a heart."* Sort of like a kindly slave owner.

They never thought we'd strike in 1981. And if we did, they never thought it would last. Actually, neither did we. We were making good money. Very good money. Probably ten times what the typical fan made. And I had gotten up to $600,000 a year.

The owners were moaning and groaning and weeping and wimpering and God, it was pathetic. They said they just didn't have any more money. They were at bottom, bone dry, tapped out.

Okay, fast-forward thirteen years and the highest paid players in the game, guys like Cal Ripken Jr. and Kirby Puckett, are now making $6 million a year. Ten times what I made. Where do you suppose the owners who didn't have any more money got that extra $5 million? Lotto?

The players said it was about freedom. The owners said it was about fairness.

The bottom line was it was about the bottom line.

Of course, some owners were more enlightened than others. I told the papers in July of '81, "Edward Bennett Williams is one of the few looking rationally at this and he knows it could be settled." He knew it; he said it; and he wasn't too popular with the other owners.

Sound familiar? One owner who looks at it realistically and knows it could be settled? One owner who says so, and isn't too popular with the others? Ed Williams in '81. Peter Angelos in '94.

In '81, a reporter asked, "Are you saying, the owners are trying to break the players' union?"

I said, "Exactly."

Exactly like '94.

The owners couldn't break the union. The players couldn't break management, either. Nobody got what they wanted. In '81 or '94.

The strike of 1981 lasted fifty-one days. It hurt the owners, it hurt the players, but mostly it hurt the game. Eventually, the game recovered. But it's like a player. Every time he's injured, it's harder to come back.

1982

Earl's Last Year. How Come I'm Not Cheering?

This was the time I had prayed for. No more aggravation. No more little pest. No more maniac-at-the-mound. What's this wet stuff coming out of my eyes? It was a lot easier when we hated each other.

At the beginning of 1982, Earl Weaver announced that it would be his last season. Some people thought that meant Weaver would manage differently that year. They thought he'd ease up. They couldn't have been more wrong.

Weaver drove the team to win, the only way he knew.

Weaver played the players who could win, as he always had.

When the front office told him to put an aging Jim Palmer in the bullpen, Earl Weaver fought it. Then he found every reason to get Palmer out of the bullpen and onto the mound.

It worked.

Jim Palmer had one more great season.

And the Orioles gave Weaver one more run for glory.

Late in '82, the Orioles made a historic drive for the American League playoffs to catch the uncatchable Milwaukee Brewers.

And the last time Earl Weaver was to pick a starting pitcher, he picked Jim Palmer.

The Bullpen

In early 1982, the *Miami Herald,* the *Baltimore Sun,* the *News American,* the *Washington Post,* and several other prominent newspapers decided my pitching future was in the past. Take your pick of headlines: PALMER TRAVELS UNCERTAIN PATH. CAN PALMER DO IT? NAGGING DOUBTS ABOUT JIM PALMER. PALMER'S PLIGHT.

Fortunately, no one ever asked a sportwriter to manage a big league baseball team.

I'd had a string of seasons, in '79, '80, and '81, that ran the gamut from bad to not bad to bad again: 10–6, 16–10, 7–8. So the odds on me being a starter in '82 were . . . bad. On top of everything else, Steve Stone, who'd won the Cy Young Award in 1980, had also gone through a lousy year in '81. So the papers were predicting a wrestling match between two senior cripples for the last spot in the rotation. Stone is an ancient thirty-five and I'm even more of a fossil at thirty-six.

God bless Earl. Stubborn Earl. Hardheaded Earl. He tells those same papers he's going to pitch me. "Age doesn't matter. Not when you're in the shape Mr. Palmer is in. He's old enough now that I can call him Mr. Palmer. At the end of the year, we'll look at the number of victories Jim has and then decide if he had a good season."

I may not be starting every fourth day like when I was in my twenties, but I'm going every six or seventh day. Then, in Anaheim, I encounter a serious pillow problem. (I think I may have neglected to include this in the "life-threatening ailments" section of my hypochondria chapter.) Anyway, I get this evil pillow and I sleep crooked and the next day my neck is like the monster that Dr. Frankenstein created only without those little pegs in the side of my throat. It's kind of frozen stiff, at a slight angle. Every time I throw the ball, my neck feels like lightning is shooting through it. It's killing me. But helping the Angels.

Evidently that was the last straw for the GM, Hank Peters. He hadn't been too keen on me anyway for going on about five years, and Earl has announced that this is his last season so Hank is not putting up with any more crap than he has to. Peters figures, indulging me is number one on the crap list he doesn't have to put up with. So he says, "Palmer is never, ever, ever going to start another game in an Orioles uniform. I've had it."

I hear what he says. I read it. I look for hidden meanings. I think I get it. To summarize, I believe, basically, he'd prefer that I not go out to the mound, particularly at the beginning of baseball games, and throw baseballs toward the plate while wearing Baltimore Orioles official clothing. I've got the gist of it. And the "never, ever, ever" part clarifies the time period in which I shouldn't do any of this. Yes, I'm sure I've got it.

Earl calls me in and says, "I'm sending you to the bullpen. But I still think you can win a lot of games." Based on that last comment, "I still think you can win a lot of games," maybe Earl didn't get it as clearly as I did.

Or maybe Hank was just kidding. Nah!

Earl just says he still believes I can start and that I can win and the best way to prove it is to get me in a lot of games. Peters didn't say anything about that.

I keep working out, going to my personal staff of doctors, doing my exercises, running, long-throwing, everything.

The trade rumors are flying like vultures over garbage. Some people are saying they're only playing me at all to show other teams I can pitch. But supposedly Earl called a meeting and Cal Ripken Sr. says he thinks I can still start and Elrod Hendricks says he thinks I can still start and Ray Miller, the pitching coach, says . . . well, he knows Earl is retiring and he wants to manage, so he says he thinks whatever Hank Peters thinks. But two out of three plus Earl isn't bad.

Meantime, the reporters from the papers who had offered

all of my premature death announcements are hammering Earl with questions/advice/annoyance. They offer insightful stuff like, "You know, Earl, if Stone is hurt and Palmer's in the bullpen, you're probably gonna need another starter."

And Earl says, for the papers and for the eyes of Hank Peters, "We don't need another starter. We got a guy who's going to the Hall of Fame sitting out in the bullpen."

But the reporters don't let up. "Well, if you start Palmer again, then you'll need somebody for long relief."

Earl fires right back, "The guy I'm starting right now instead of Palmer, is Sammy Stewart, who is the best long reliever in the game." Which at the time is more of a prediction than a fact but one which comes true shortly thereafter. Sammy Stewart ends up being one of the very best long relievers ever.

And this is the year I decided not to talk to the press. At least the in-town press. Which may not be a big deal for anyone else but for somebody who has a weakness for the sound of his own voice and his own opinions and the last word and the word after the last word—somebody like me—it's killing me, but I'm sticking to it. Even I am finally tired of reading about this guy Palmer and his aches and pains and complaints and his salary and blah-blah-blah.

I just play baseball. I come in for relief almost every two days. I pitch okay. And finally I get to start. In Texas. We get a 9–0 lead going into the ninth inning.

Now I haven't gone nine innings, or eight, for that matter, in I don't know how long. And my strikes start drifting into balls, higher and higher. And I come out. We win but I don't finish and Dempsey, who's catching, says something about how I should have finished. Why, I don't know. He's a great catcher but he's always been strung tighter than Andre Agassi's tennis racket.

Example: He would beat himself up all the time for not hitting .300, so one time I'm sitting with him and I say, why are you doing this to yourself? He says he's got to hit .300. I say, what's your lifetime average, and he says, it's like .239, .260, and now it's .240. I say, Rick, why don't you just say to yourself, anything I hit over .240 is like a bonus? He goes wild and says, "Are you calling me a .240 hitter?!"

So this wired-too-tight guy, Dempsey, thinks I should have finished the game. I didn't finish it but we won. I won. And it was my 250th win.

I won my next eleven games. And the headlines from those same papers that were delivering my eulogies started to change. THE FALL AND RISE OF JIM PALMER. IT'S PALMER OF OLD, DESPITE ADVERSITY.

My favorite line was from John Steadman of the *News American:* SILENCE IS GOLDEN FOR PALMER. I didn't talk; I pitched.

But Earl talked. Stubborn, hardheaded, retiring-in-fact-but-not-retiring-in-personal–style Earl talked plenty. He went right back to the reporters with his I-told-you-so. "I said look at Palmer's record at the end of the season. I said back then he had sixty more wins in him, didn't I?"

I started starting again. *In spite of what Hank Peters said.* The team is winning and I'm winning. I ended up 15–5. *In spite of what Hank Peters said.* I know I put that line in twice. It's for emphasis, Hank.

And Earl, thanks.

Parting Is Such Sweet Sorrow

Baseball is a business of wins, losses, stats, and attendance, but ballplayers are a lot more emotional than people think. Sure, we care about RBIs, ERAs, bonuses, and contracts, but we care about the human side of things, too. Like when your manager decides to hang it up after fifteen years. We each had deep, personal feelings about Earl's departure. How would we struggle on without him, and what time would the party start to celebrate our new freedom?

He had been with us inning after inning, game after game. And now, in a day or so, he'd be gone. Just like that. No more Earl Weaver. Some people wept . . . and some even in sadness.

Sure, we had our bitches and gripes about him. Yeah, he drove us to the brink of insanity and made us beg for electric shock treatments. Okay, he could go on psycho tirades like a crazed postal worker. Yes, he had a Mafia hitman's temper and a little less sympathy than Satan. So he was despised, hated, and loathed by all the umpires who didn't want him killed. And okay, certain ballplayers had Earl voodoo dolls that had no more room for pins.

He'd be gone, and each of us would have to deal with the loss in our own way. There were serious things to think about. Like whether we'd get a tall manager to take his place or if they'd clean all the old chicken bones out of his desk.

The truth is, it wasn't funny. It was hard.

It was 1982 and we were in the race right up to the last game of the season. We had a great team. Gary Roenicke, John Lowenstein, Rick Dempsey, Richie Dauer, John Shelby, Al Bumbry. We had a great hitting, Gold Glove–fielding first baseman, Eddie Murray. It was Cal Ripken's first year and the beginning of what was going to turn into his consecutive game streak. We had great pitching with Scotty McGregor, Mike Flanagan, Dennis Martinez, and the hope of the future, Storm Davis. We had "Cy Young" in Flanagan, who had just won it in '79, and "Cy Old" in me, who'd won it three times before.

Milwaukee had this big lead on everybody and a fantastic team. But somehow we just kept gaining on them—seven and a half ahead and then six and then only three—right up to the end of the season. It was a TV network's dream. We had to win the last four-game series to catch them and beat them.

We won the first of four, the second of four, and then Storm Davis pitched the third, the one that would tie it all up if we could win. The thing about Storm was you could practically program him, tell him what to throw and he'd just throw it. I talked him through the whole Brewers lineup, including Robin Yount, who was almost unstoppable, and Storm just went out and did it like a pitching machine. And the Orioles did their part with between nine and thirteen runs in every one of those last three games.

The division title that Milwaukee supposedly ran away with is now up for grabs. And it comes down to the last game of the season, Earl Weaver's last game for the Orioles. (Until later when Edward Bennett Williams brought him back, but "later" hadn't happened yet.) High drama.

Whoever wins the game that day goes to the American League playoffs. And maybe beyond. But after that, it's the Orioles without Earl Weaver.

I'm pitching. And I've had a good year. A sort of miracle year. I was sent to the bullpen "forever" but managed to cut "forever" a few months short. I went from 2–3 to 15–4. I won thirteen of my last fourteen. I slipped and slid around in some rainy games and I've pitched over 3,600 innings, so at thirty-six years old I'm a little tired, and I got tackled by Danny Ford at Tiger Stadium shagging flies, but I want to pitch and I want to win.

At the time I might not have admitted it, but I guess I was as nervous before that game as I was before the Series in '66 or '70. I really wanted it for the come-from-behind of it all and for the team and for . . . okay, I had a lump in my throat for the maniac I'd been playing under for all those years. We all did. We wanted to win it for Earl, for all he'd done for us, with us, at us, by us, and to us.

We were in the clubhouse before the game. It was almost eerily silent; no joking or hollering; a group of men trying to act like they're cool as ice while they're struggling to hold their guts inside.

Earl calls us over to talk. We sit on the locker room stools. Where we'd sat a million times. To listen to his sage pregame strategy and his ranting, raging postgame hollering fest.

Earl gets us together and he says, "I want to tell all you guys how proud I am of you. This is going to be my last game as an Oriole manager. And you've all made my job easy." (I'm not positive but he might have said, "You've all made my job easier except for Palmer.")

And then Earl gets real quiet and almost whispers, "One more thing," and takes this gigantic pause. Finally he says, "I don't care what happens today, I'm telling you guys, you had a great year."

Dauer, our second baseman, lets out this gigantic sigh of relief and says, "Whew! I thought for a minute you were gonna tell us you changed your mind and you weren't going to retire." Everybody laughs and lets out all the emotions we had crammed inside. We're ready to play our final game.

But first it's Earl Weaver's day at Memorial Stadium. The crowd is really charged. Everybody in the stands was with us. During that last run, they'd stay in their seats after the games were over and just shout for the game heroes like they do for Broadway curtain calls, and they'd sit there until Lowenstein or Dauer or whoever finally came out and tipped his cap.

So now EBW, Edward Bennett Williams, who knew how to do a summation for the jury, addresses all fifty-two thousand of this jury. He's in front of the microphone and he's getting that God-echo that he never got even on his best day in a courtroom and he announces they're retiring Earl's number. The crowd does a two-minute long ocean roar!

Then he throws three straight, reverberating strikes:
"Earl, we love you!–love you!–love you!" Bigger Roar!
"We'll always love you, Earl!-Earl!-Earl!" Even Bigger Roar!

"You will always be loved in Bal-ti-more!-more!-more!"
Deafening Roar!

A tough act to follow. It turned out to really be Earl's last game. Everything that worked on Yount the game before didn't work on Sunday. I threw him a low and away fastball and he put it high and away into the right field stands. He did it the next time up, too. Dempsey said we've got to throw to him up and in, but some days you just know that guys who are hitting can even hit the pitches they aren't supposed to be able to hit and Yount did, over the left field wall. By the time I left it was 4–1.

We threw everything at them. Flanagan from the bullpen, then Tippy Martinez. We didn't get our nine to thirteen runs, but they did. We lost, 10–2.

But you wouldn't have known it from the crowd. They just stayed in their seats, chanting and shouting, "Orioles! Orioles!" until we came out, every single one of us, and finally Earl. He tipped his hat.

They played the ABC tape of it over and over, with Howard Cosell doing that nasal, stretched-out, sing-songy, Cosell voice: "Thee Er-uhl of Bal-tee-more. They love . . . troo-lee love . . . this man, Er-uhl Weeev-ver! A man *of* the people. The Weeeve! One *of* a kind. A baseball gar-rate!"

We kidded about Earl. We suffered with him. He made us nuts. We won with him. Dauer was right, we were afraid he'd change his mind and stay. And we were afraid to play without him.

He didn't show his feelings like, say, Sparky Anderson. When the Tigers came from behind to steal the race from the Blue Jays in '87, Sparky ran to the mound and hugged and kissed Frank Tanana. If Earl ever hugged and kissed me I'd know he had to be doing it to win a bet.

Maybe that's what went wrong that last game. Earl practically made us cry in the locker room with that speech. It

Earl's Last Year. How Come I'm Not Cheering?   **157**

was so . . . so . . . human. So unlike Earl. We just didn't know how to play for a guy who acted like that. Just when we needed him ripping up his hat and telling us to stop fucking up, there he was, doing a perfect imitation of a . . . a . . . a person.

It was your fault, Earl, you . . . you . . . goddamn human being, you!

Five Words

"If it's okay with Jim." That one comment, made by Earl Weaver during the 1982 American League playoffs, explains a lot. From 1969 to the last Oriole game of 1982, other than whether my arm felt good enough to pitch, he never asked if something was "okay with Jim" before he did it. He never questioned, doubted, worried, wondered, pondered, daydreamed, fantasized, or wasted one extra breath contemplating if something he wanted to do was "okay with Jim."

Everything he did, he did to win. Period. W-I-N. End of philosophy. Forget what I thought or what any other player thought, or for the most part, what the front office and the owners thought. All they paid him to do was win. All they'd fire him for was losing.

And that was why we fought. Period. I wanted what Earl wanted. To win. I thought my way was the right way. He thought his way was right. Who should pitch first in the playoffs. Which lineup to go with. What to throw to a pull hitter with two men on. When to bring in a reliever. Left- or right-handed. Everything.

But Earl was the manager. So Earl got to be right. And I wasn't wrong; I was less than wrong. I didn't count. And that really pissed me off. Which pissed Earl off.

So we fought some more. All about winning.

That was the miscalculation ABC made when they asked

Earl and me to join Keith Jackson on the broadcast team for the 1982 playoffs. They figured they would (1) answer the dyed-in-the-flannel baseball nuts who say networks never put knowlegeable guys in the booth but always go for the TV talking head, perfect diction, banter boys, and (2) get Earl Weaver and Jim Palmer's legendary love-hate-scream relationship on national TV to liven up baseball, which has been known to have its comatosely dull moments.

They got number one but not number two. Earl and I had nothing to fight about. We couldn't win. We'd already lost. We weren't playing.

We were just two guys getting paid to watch a baseball game. And talk about it. Like civilized, savvy, experienced baseball veterans. He didn't call me a baby. I didn't accuse him of being pigheaded. He didn't propose some dumb pitching rotation that he thought could somehow win. I wasn't part of that dumb pitching rotation that could never win. He didn't slam any doors. I didn't demand to be traded. It wasn't our game. It was someone else's. The final score didn't matter.

So when Dennis Lewin, the ABC producer, asked me if I wanted to have dinner after the Milwaukee game and I said "sure," and then he asked Earl if he wanted to go and Earl said, "If it's okay with Jim," that told the whole story. Earl wasn't the manager. I wasn't the player. We were the same. Equals.

Earl knew it. I was a little slower. I had thirteen years of a whole other relationship. And except for a few Saturdays on the golf course, we were manager-player, in that order.

Earl just instantly knew everything was different in a broadcast booth, off the field, out of uniform, working for a network instead of a team owner, with nobody keeping score, at least not our score.

Me, it took a little longer. I had to be revived when he asked if it was "okay with Jim."

Things would never be the same between us. It wasn't about winning anymore. That took awhile for me to get used to.

And Another Thing

In early '83, the season after Earl called it quits, the team was on our United chartered plane flying someplace or other. When they delivered the meals, the usual shrimp cocktail wasn't there. Rich Dauer, who's sitting up front, yells out, "Hey, where's the shrimp?"

Flanagan, sitting next to me four rows back, without missing a beat, says, "He's retired and playing golf in Florida."

Even after the body left, his presence lingered. Especially around my locker. Reporters couldn't resist.

Did I realize that 245 of my 268 career wins were under Earl?
"Of course, I realized it. Earl reminded me all the time."

What would I miss most about him?
"His obsession with winning. Did you think I was going to say it was his compassion?"

Did I know he said, he wished I'd quit trying to be funny and cute?
"Yeah, I read that, but since he retired now only one of us can be funny and cute."

Nobody could get used to Palmer without Weaver and Weaver without Palmer. The feuds. The fights. The he said–I said–who saids . . .

A sportswriter found Earl coming off the golf course one day and told him that I gave up three runs in only two innings in an intrasquad game. Earl said, "Did he blame me?"

Almost like he missed it. I know I did.

People Skills

Earl stuck by his players long after other managers and owners and coaches and players and the guy's own wife and kids had given up on him. He put guys into the lineup because of what they once did, not what they could still do. He'd make out the lineup, leave a guy off, then drive to the ballpark and, on the way, remember all the great things that guy had done once upon a time, and by the time Earl arrived at the ballpark, the guy was back in the lineup.

He was fiercely loyal to his players. He cared about them. He stood by them.

He just never got to know them.

He could be around a guy for ten seasons, run into him at the ATM machine, and have nothing to say to him but "too bad about that time you missed the take sign." It never occurred to him to ask about the weather. He just didn't see players as regular people. He saw them as second basemen or shortstops or relief pitchers. Whether he was in uniform or not.

Once, down in Florida, the year after Earl retired, he walked into the Miami Stadium locker room. I'm hanging upside down like a bat from the bars in the locker room, stretching my back. Evidently Earl didn't see me or didn't recognize me since I wasn't right side up or maybe he thought I was a very tall bat.

But he did see Dennis Martinez, a very talented pitcher who had played with the Orioles and for Earl for a long time. Martinez is getting some soup and he looks up and there's Earl.

Now he and Martinez had been through a lot together. Earl managed him through his early, promising but troubled years in the game. He'd seen Dennis on top and winning and pretty low and losing. In fact, Earl knew Dennis's career inside and out, but after all those seasons, he didn't really know Dennis.

So, this is the first time Earl will ever say anything to the guy on a personal level, a nonbaseball level, non-walk-out-to-the-mound level, non-soak-your-arm-in-the-whirlpool level, non-if-you-have-another-lousy-game-pack-your-stuff-and-get-a-bus-ticket-to-Triple-A level.

What will Earl say? How's your wife? What's new with the kids? What'd you do in the off-season? Who do you like in the presidential race? Nice haircut? How's your lawn? Seen any good movies?

None of the above.

Earl looks at Martinez and says, "How's your curveball?"

Martinez mumbles something into his soup that makes the noodles cringe and wanders away.

Me? I just hang there, amazed. After all that time, all Earl could do is ask about a guy's curveball. It's not that Earl didn't like his guys. He did. He even loved them. In his way. Which was to put them in the lineup.

1983 and beyond
The Last Chapter. Maybe.

**I still talk to Earl Weaver now and then. We don't yell
and scream and curse anymore. But hey, all good
things must come to an end.**

*Joe Altobelli became Baltimore's manager in 1983. The
Orioles won the American League pennant and went on to
face the Philadelphia Phillies in the World Series.*

*A lot of the players on that Orioles team were Earl
Weaver's players, including Jim Palmer. Altobelli put Palmer
into Game 3 of the Series to relieve Mike Flanagan against
Steve Carlton. The Orioles went on to win that game and to
take the World Series.*

*In 1984, Jim Palmer stepped off the mound for the last
time. He decided not to pursue his career with any other team
and, instead, concentrated on his broadcasting and commercial future.*

*Edward Bennett Williams, then the owner of the Orioles,
brought Earl Weaver out of retirement to manage during the
1985 season, the first season he had ever managed Baltimore
without Jim Palmer on his pitching staff. Earl managed
through 1986, then retired for good.*

*In 1990, in his first year of eligibility, Palmer was voted
into the Hall of Fame in Cooperstown, New York. Earl
Weaver flew up from Florida to give his congratulations.*

*In 1991, at the age of forty-five, Jim Palmer made the
decision to try to pitch for the Orioles again. This time it
would have been without Earl Weaver as his manager. Midway through spring training, Jim retired for good.*

The "Re" Word

Earl hung it up in '82.

I hung it up in '84.

In between, in 1983, we won the division, the American League pennant, and the World Series. I might have been one of the first to say, see, we can win without the lunatic at the controls.

But I'd also be one of the first to say, we won with a team Earl put together. Joe Altobelli did what a good manager should do. Not fuck up a winner.

And I managed to pitch one of those World Series wins in '83.

For me, 1984, the year, was a lot like *1984*, the book. The end of things as they had been.

I retired.

Okay, I was released. It was one of those "re" words. On May 17, 1984, I went in front of the press and cried. Almost nineteen years to the day after my first major league victory, I said good-bye. Or I tried.

Mr. Cool couldn't stay cool. Mr. Rational couldn't rationalize. Mr. Hypochondria didn't have a thing broken except his spirit.

When I drove to the press conference, I came down Walther Boulevard where I had lived my first year in Baltimore, and it was like a memory avalanche of all the things that had happened to me since I'd been there, all the teams and years I'd been part of, the All-Star games and the World Series and raising my kids there and being part of the community. And I'd always had the luxury, even after the divorce, of living in the same neighborhood as my kids and having them around when I was home, having breakfast with them in the morning, and them coming by on their way to school or on the way back from school, before I went to the ballpark.

And then I started imagining, picturing me going to pitch for another team now, in another city, at this point not just in my career but in my life. These things I knew and loved and even took for granted, they were all going to end. I was thirty-eight, and did I want to give all that up to see if there was another season in me?

That's what was going through my mind when I went to face the writers and cameras.

I could barely talk. My opening line was, "I still think I can pitch. I have the desire to pitch." But I wasn't sure I meant it anymore.

I stopped. I got myself back together and said, "I really don't want to be here, and I'm going to leave if this gets too emotional." And it did.

I tried to make a joke about the whole thing being my way of getting out of this exhibition game that no one wanted to go to in Rochester, but everybody in the room knew I was two eye blinks from a tear flood.

My voice cracked and I said to the TV guys, "I hope you have a lot of tape." Then I just choked up again. "There's no way I can talk. Bear with me. I'm gonna leave."

And I walked away.

Naturally, the press tracked Earl down in Florida. He said almost the same thing I did. "No words could have come out of my mouth today. If there was one thing I am extremely grateful for, it's that I didn't have to be there. I'm glad I could be a thousand miles away. Hell, I'm really sad."

They kept asking me what I was going to do. Maybe I'd try to play for another team this season. Maybe next season. Or be an analyst for ABC. Or a pitching coach. And I had an endorsement contract with Jockey. And maybe . . .

How did I know what I'd do? I had never had a job. I'd been playing games, literally, since I was a kid. I got paid, but it wasn't work. I got to throw baseballs while other people

The Last Chapter. Maybe.   **165**

drove through rush hour. Now, I was done "playing." Finally, I was going to be a grown-up. Or try.

And they kept asking me if I wanted a Jim Palmer Day. I kept saying no. In 1985, they asked if I'd do it for my number one cause, cystic fibrosis. I couldn't say no.

The City of Baltimore put up a Jim Palmer Corner, Twenty-second Street and Charles, complete with its own sign. Mayor Schaefer officially "gave" me the Oriole strike zone. Edward Bennett Williams retired number 22 and my jersey.

They gave me the keys to a boat and I told Earl, "You can be the captain anytime you want but I have to warn you. There aren't any life preservers."

Davey Leonhard talked about me. "It's a grand event befitting a gentleman and a gentle man."

I was touched.

Then he went on, "But I don't want to give you the idea that he's perfect because number one, he introduced me to my wife and number two, he introduced me to golf."

Rick Dempsey said, "The only thing I have against Palmer is he left me here by myself to argue with Earl Weaver." See, Earl was back managing again. Williams had brought him out of retirement.

My daughters, Jamie and Kelly, were there. My friends were there. My old teammates were there. Ralph Salvon was there. My dad, Max, threw out the first ball before the game.

And when it was all over, we had raised $125,000 for cystic fibrosis.

It was a good day. And a hard day. I cried again. And I said what I felt. "You can retire a uniform but you can't retire your heart."

Then, a few years later, came the Hall of Fame. You can say to yourself, I won't think about it. Or you can say, it's just an award. You can say anything you want to yourself to make it seem like it's not so important, but it's all lies.

It's really important. It's great. It's an honor among honors. On August 6 of 1990, I was inducted into the Hall of Fame in Cooperstown, New York. Me and Joe Morgan of the Reds. In our first year of eligibility.

The night of the vote, January 9, 1990, we had all gone over to my friend Hersh Pachino's restaurant, the Orchard Inn. I asked Hersh, "What if I don't make it?"

He said, "We'll just do this again next year."

Jack Lang of the Baseball Writers Association had asked where we'd be, and somehow instead of getting the phone number for the Orchard Inn, he got the number for Obrycki's Crab House. At seven P.M. when we were supposed to hear, there was no call. At eight P.M., still no call. At 8:30, nothing.

I was engaged to Joni, and her son P.J. was there. Around nine P.M. P.J. says, "Doesn't look too good, Jim."

Then the phone rang. They hand it to me. Jack Lang says, "The bad news is, 33 writers didn't vote for you. The good news is, 411 did."

Holy shit!

That's second only to Bob Feller. And, not to sound like a little kid, but *Feller's in the Hall of Fame!* Oh, wait a minute. So was I! Me and Joe Morgan. And, by the way, I only threw two leadoff home runs in my career, one to Tommy Agee of the Mets in the '69 World Series and the other to my Hall of Fame–mate, Joe Morgan.

Of course, nobody was going to let that day go by without asking me about Earl Weaver and my career. "I'm sure Earl would say he got me into the Hall of Fame. And maybe he did. I'm sure he made me better by coming to the mound and saying, 'Don't turn around and look in the bullpen because there's no one out there any better than you.'"

And then they got to Earl and just begged him for one last, feisty, crusty, cranky, four-letter Weaver-ism. They told Earl, say whatever you want about Palmer, and Earl did. "He made it easy for a pitching coach and a manager to be successful."

Pretty nice comments for guys who were supposed to despise each other.

We didn't. We just loved to play baseball. And hated to lose. And we never quit.

Maybe that's why in 1991, at the age of forty-five, I tried my comeback. I wanted to see if I could be like Nolan Ryan was to the game or what George Blanda was to football. Even Earl said I had retired too early.

I couldn't throw ninety-five miles an hour anymore. The best I could do was eighty. My control wasn't bad. But it was too late. By March 12, I knew. I told Frank Robinson, who was managing, I pulled a hamstring and it was over. Imagine, an injury, of all things.

My comeback never came back. Neither did Earl's. There was just something missing. When he came back, I was gone. When I came back, he was gone. Maybe, just maybe, we needed each other.

Earl said, when he heard about my intention to return, "No question, he stopped pitching too soon. If I had still been there I would have fought it." That was awful nice of him to say.

Then he added, "But I probably would have had another big fight with Jim in the process, because I would have asked him to use his slider."

He *still* wants me to throw a *goddamn slider!?* Just like he told me to throw to Beniquez in 1978. When he said, everybody in this fucking league is throwing fucking sliders to this .166 hitter! And I refused to throw that dumb pitch! The pitch that Earl got Don Stanhouse to throw. And Beniquez smashed it off the wall with the bases loaded. *That slider!* It's just like Dave McNally said, "The only thing Earl knew about pitching was that he couldn't hit it." Who is *he* to tell *me* what to throw?! Throw the fucking pitch and stop whining, he'd say. I can still hear him. Bitching about the goddamn umps and kicking dirt and calling me a baby! *A slider?! A goddamn slider!*

God, we loved to win.